JOURNAL FOR THE STUDY OF THE PSEUDEPIGRAPHA SUPPLEMENT SERIES
31

Sheffield Academic Press

Jewish Local Patriotism and Self-Identification in the Graeco-Roman Period

edited by
Siân Jones
& Sarah Pearce

Journal for the Study of the Pseudepigrapha
Supplement Series 31

Copyright © 1998 Sheffield Academic Press

Published by Sheffield Academic Press Ltd
Mansion House
19 Kingfield Road
Sheffield S11 9AS
England

Printed on acid-free paper in Great Britain
by Bookcraft Ltd
Midsomer Norton, Bath

British Library Cataloguing in Publication Data

A catalogue record for this book is available
from the British Library

ISBN 1-85075-832-8

CONTENTS

GRAHAM HARVEY

ACKNOWLEDGMENTS

This volume has its origins in a one-day conference, 'Jewish Local Patriotism and Self-Identification in the Graeco-Roman Period', held under the auspices of the Parkes Library and the Hartley Institute at the University of Southampton on 28 March 1995. It includes papers presented at the original conference together with some additional contributions to the original programme. The editors would like to express their thanks to the Hartley Institute for a grant which made this event possible, to Chris Woolgar and Tony Kushner for their advice and assistance, and to Martin Goodman for his encouragement and support of this project. Special thanks are due to all those who contributed to and participated in the original conference, the first of its kind at the University of Southampton.

Siân Jones and Sarah Pearce
The Parkes Centre for the Study of Jewish/Non-Jewish Relations,
University of Southampton

ABBREVIATIONS

Aeg	*Aegyptus*
ANRW	Hildegard Temporini and Wolfgang Haase (eds.), *Aufstieg und Niedergang der römischen Welt: Geschichte und Kultur Roms im Spiegel der neueren Forschung* (Berlin: W de Gruyter, 1972–)
ASOR	American Schools of Oriental Research
BA	*Biblical Archaeologist*
BCH	*Bulletin de Correspondance Hellénique*
BJPES	*Bulletin of the Jewish Palestine Exploration Society*
BJS	Brown Judaic Studies
BZAW	Beihefte zur *Zeitschrift für die alttestamentliche Wissenschaft*
CBQ	*Catholic Biblical Quarterly*
C. Theo.	*Codex Theodosianus*
CII I	*Corpus inscriptionum judaicarum,* I
CII I²	reprinted version of *CII* I, with 'Prolegomenon' by B. Lifshitz
CII II	*Corpus inscriptionum judaicarum,* II
CPJ I–III	V. Tcherikover and A. Fuks (eds.), *Corpus papyrorum judaicarum* (3 vols.; Cambridge, MA: Harvard University Press, 1957–64)
DJD	Discoveries in the Judaean Desert
EncJud	*Encyclopaedia Judaica*
HAT	Handbuch zum Alten Testament
HTR	*Harvard Theological Review*
HUCA	*Hebrew Union College Annual*
ICC	International Critical Commentary
IEJ	*Israel Exploration Journal*
JAOS	*Journal of the American Oriental Society*
JBL	*Journal of Biblical Literature*
JGA	J. Reynolds and R. Tannenbaum (eds.), *Jews and God-Fearers at Aphrodisias* (Cambridge: Cambridge Philological Society, 1987)
JIWE	D. Noy (ed.), *Jewish Inscriptions of Western Europe* (2 vols.; Cambridge: Cambridge University Press, 1993, 1995)
JJS	*Journal of Jewish Studies*

JQR	*Jewish Quarterly Review*
JSJ	*Journal for the Study of Judaism in the Persian, Hellenistic and Roman Period*
JSOT	*Journal for the Study of the Old Testament*
JSOTSup	*Journal for the Study of the Old Testament,* Supplement Series
JSS	*Journal of Semitic Studies*
KAT	Kommentar zum Alten Testament
KTU	M. Dietrich, O. Loretz, J. Sanmartín (eds.), *Die Keilalphabetischen Texte aus Ugarit: Einschliesslich der keilalphabetischen Texte ausserhalb Ugarits* (Kevelaer: Butzon & Bercker; Neukirchen-Vluyn: Neukirchner Verlag, 1976)
LCL	Loeb Classical Library
NTOA	Novum Testamentum et orbis antiquus
NRSV	New Revised Standard Version
OED	*Oxford English Dictionary* (Oxford: Clarendon Press, 1989)
OTL	Old Testament Library
REJ	*Revue des études juives*
SBLSP	SBL Seminar Papers
SJLA	Studies in Judaism in Late Antiquity
SPB	Studia postbiblica
SVF	*Stoicorum Veterum Fragmenta* (Fragments of the Early Stoics, ed. H. von Arnim)
TDNT	Gerhard Kittel and Gerhard Friedrich (eds.), *Theological Dictionary of the New Testament* (trans. Geoffrey W. Bromiley; 10 vols.; Grand Rapids: Eerdmans, 1964–)
WBC	Word Biblical Commentary

LIST OF CONTRIBUTORS

Richard Coggins, formerly of the Department of Theology and Religious Studies, Kings College, University of London

Lester L. Grabbe, Department of Theology, University of Hull

Graham Harvey, School of Religious Studies, King Alfred's College, Winchester

Siân Jones, Honorary Parkes Fellow, formerly of the Department of Archaeology, University of Southampton

David Noy, Department of Classics, University of Wales, Lampeter

Sarah Pearce, Department of History, University of Southampton

Joshua Schwartz, Ingeborg Rennert Center for Jerusalem Studies, Bar Ilan University, Israel

INTRODUCTION: JEWISH LOCAL IDENTITIES AND PATRIOTISM IN THE GRAECO-ROMAN PERIOD

Sarah Pearce and Siân Jones

...for Jews everywhere Israel has become a symbol, of the life of the Jewish people, of unity within diversity, and, above all, hope.[1]

The centrality of the idea of the Land of Israel[2] for many Jews today and throughout history is unquestionable. The Land and especially its Temple city of Jerusalem have been at the centre of much Jewish reflection in connection with the divine promises of the Land in the Pentateuch, devotion to the Temple cult, eschatological expectations

1.   N. de Lange, *Judaism* (Oxford: Oxford University Press, 1986), p. 150.
2.   The essays in this volume embrace a broad period (from the beginnings of the Second Temple period in the sixth century BCE to the fifth century CE) when the territory which includes the site of the Second Temple varied considerably both in dimension and in its official and unofficial designations. Furthermore, this region (or parts of it) has been accorded a variety of names by modern scholars including the Land of Israel, the Land, Judaea, Palestine and Syro-Palestine, all of which may contain latent political implications in the contemporary period, as discussed by a number of authors such as J. Parkes, *Whose Land? A History of the Peoples of Palestine* (New York: Taplinger, 1970), see the 'Preface'; and K. Whitelam, *The Invention of Ancient Israel: The Silencing of Palestinian History* (London: Routledge, 1996), pp. 55-56. For the purposes of a broad designation we use here the expressions 'Land of Israel' or 'the Land' (individual contributors to this volume may use more specific terms relevant to the particular contexts and texts with which they are concerned). The expressions 'Land of Israel' or 'the Land' follow the conventional designations within Scripture and Jewish tradition generally of the territory promised to the ancestors, and the location of the Temple: they are, therefore, particularly appropriate for expressing the idea of the Land in Jewish consciousness in antiquity, with which this book is primarily concerned. It should be noted, however, that this designation should not be taken as implying the existence of 'an Israel' as an *actual* territorial or political entity that persisted throughout the period covered by this volume. No single term exists that adequately denotes the territory/territories in question as a political entity during the whole of this period.

centring on Jerusalem and the Land,[3] and as the focus of the longing expressed by those who have seen themselves as exiles, from the author of Psalm 137 onwards. The Land has also been a territory governed as a Jewish state, with varying degrees of autonomy, at different times, most recently in the form of the modern State of Israel. Largely because of these two factors, it has played an important role in the construction of Jewish identities. As W.D. Davies points out in his study of *The Territorial Dimension of Judaism*, the 'complexities, paradoxes, and obscurities' of this territorial theme in Judaism and Jewish life cannot be overemphasized.[4] Indeed, these complexities have been heightened in the last hundred years with the development of the Zionist movement and the establishment of the modern state of Israel, making the question of the historical relationship between the Jewish people and the Land of Israel/Palestine one of pressing political importance.[5] Yet despite its significance, this question has been relatively neglected, at least where it applies to antiquity. Recent decades have seen a handful of studies that focus on the territorial dimension in early Judaism.[6] Most of these studies have, however, been largely concerned with the significance of 'the Land' as a religious concept. There have been very few historical studies which explore the social, political and cultural manifestations of this territorial dimension for

3. E.P. Sanders, *Judaism: Practice and Belief 63 BCE–66 CE* (London: SCM Press; Philadelphia: Trinity Press International, 1994), pp. 289-93.

4. W.D. Davies, *The Territorial Dimension of Judaism* (Berkeley: University of California Press, 1982), pp. xv-xvi.

5. For example, Y. Zerubavel, *Recovered Roots: Collective Memory and the Making of Israeli National Tradition* (Chicago: University of Chicago Press, 1995), p. 15 and *passim*.

6. See, for example, in addition to Davies, *The Territorial Dimension*, G. Strecker (ed.), *Das Land Israel in biblischer Zeit* (Göttingen: Vandenhoeck & Ruprecht, 1983); L. Hoffman (ed.), *The Land of Israel: Jewish Perspectives* (Notre Dame: University of Notre Dame Press, 1986); D. Fiensy, *The Social History of Palestine in the Herodian Period: The Land is Mine* (Lewiston, NY; Queenston; Lampeter: Edwin Mellen Press, 1991); focusing on the Land in Christian tradition, R. Wilken, *The Land Called Holy* (New Haven: Yale University Press, 1992); B. Halpern-Amaru, *Rewriting the Bible: Land Covenant in Postbiblical Jewish Literature* (Valley Forge, PA: Trinity Press International, 1994). There have been many more studies that focus specifically on Jerusalem, see most recently M. Poorthuis and C. Safrai (eds.), *The Centrality of Jerusalem: Historical Perspectives* (Kampen: Kok, 1996); K. Jenner and G. Wiegers (eds.), *Jerusalem als heilige stad: Religieuze voorstelling en geloofspraktijk* (Kampen: Kok, 1996).

specific Jewish communities living in diverse contexts in antiquity.[7]

The subject of Jewish identity and Judaism during the Persian, Greek and Roman periods has become the focus of active and productive research over the last few decades. We have seen a move away from the understanding of Judaism and Jewish identity as normative, homogeneous phenomena, to the establishment of a new perspective in which the '[t]he cartography appears much messier'.[8] Notions of 'essence' and homogeneity have been abandoned and an alternative model has been widely adopted which stresses the existence of a plurality of Judaisms and Jewish identities in antiquity that made up complex and variegated social phenomena in both the Land of Israel and the Diaspora.[9]

---

7. Exceptions include, in addition to some of the essays in Poorthuis and Safrai (eds.), *The Centrality of Jerusalem*; Fiensy, *Social History*; D. Mendels, *The Land of Israel as a Political Concept in Hasmonean Literature: Recourse to History in Second Century BC claims to the Holy Land* (Tübingen: J.C.B. Mohr [Paul Siebeck], 1987); I. Gafni, 'Expressions and Types of "Local Patriotism" among the Jews of Sasanian Babylonia', in S. Shaked and A. Netzer (eds.), *Irano-Judaica* (Jerusalem: Ben-Zvi Institute, 1990), II, pp. 63-71; I. Gafni, *Land, Centre and Diaspora: Jewish Perceptions of National Dispersion and Land Centrality in Late Antiquity* (JSPSup, 21; Sheffield: Sheffield Academic Press, 1997).

8. J.Z. Smith, 'Fences and Neighbours: Some Contours of Early Judaism', in W.S. Green (ed.), *Approaches to Ancient Judaism* (Chico, CA: Scholars Press, 1980), II, pp. 1-25 (19-20).

9. The literature on this question is increasingly abundant: on the varieties of Jewish experience and attitudes generally see M. Smith, 'Palestinian Judaism in the First Century', in M. Davis (ed.), *Israel: Its Role in Civilization* (New York: The Seminary Israel Institute of the Jewish Theological Seminary, 1956), pp. 67-81; R. Kraft, 'The Multiform Jewish Heritage of Early Christianity', in J. Neusner (ed.), *Christianity, Judaism and Other Greco-Roman Cults* (Leiden: E.J. Brill, 1975), III, pp. 174-99; J. Dunn, 'Judaism in the Land of Israel in the First Century', in J. Neusner (ed.), *Judaism in Late Antiquity* (Leiden: E.J. Brill, 1995), II, pp. 229-61. On the diversity of Diaspora Jewish experience see V. Tcherikover, 'Prolegomena', in V. Tcherikover and A. Fuks (eds.), *Corpus Papyrorum Judaicarum* (Jerusalem: Magnes Press; Cambridge, MA: Harvard University Press, 1957), I, pp. 1-112; J. Collins, *Between Athens and Jerusalem: Jewish Identity in the Hellenistic Diaspora* (New York: Crossroad, 1986); P. Trebilco, *Jewish Communities in Asia Minor* (Cambridge: Cambridge University Press, 1991); J. Overman, 'The Diaspora in the Modern Study of Ancient Judaism', in J. Overman and R. MacLennan (eds.), *Diaspora Jews and Judaism: Essays in Honor of, and in Dialogue with, A. Thomas Kraabel* (Atlanta: Scholars Press, 1992), pp. 63-78; S.J.D. Cohen and E.S. Frerichs (eds.), *Diasporas in Antiquity* (Atlanta: Scholars

An important aspect of charting the varieties of Jewish experience and perspective in antiquity is exploring the extent to which our sources reflect identification and affiliation with the Land and, at the same time, to consider the evidence for their expressing a sense of patriotism towards local authorities and communities. This enterprise requires careful attention to the effect of ideological presuppositions which assume, whether from benign motives or not, the controlling influence of Jerusalem on the Diaspora. As A.T. Kraabel has shown, the 'questionable assumptions' in previous scholarship on the Roman Jewish Diaspora included the view that

> Diaspora Jewry was seen to be monolithic, interconnected and even directly controlled from Palestine... No matter how long they had lived in the west, Jews were not to be trusted because their overriding loyalty and allegiance remained firmly attached to the Holy Land. The extreme and diabolical form of this view was represented by G. Kittel and his colleagues of the *Forschungen zur Judenfrage*; they christened the monolith *das antike Weltjudentum*... More benign reflections of this image are still available... particularly in the assumption that the western Diaspora was administered or controlled by travelling rabbis... from Palestine.[10]

The notion that Jews in the Graeco-Roman period shared a common devotion and sense of loyalty towards the Land of Israel is a widespread assumption in earlier scholarship.[11] Such an approach is often bound up with the idea that the Jews of the Diaspora normally saw themselves as living in an alien environment (another of the 'questionable assumptions' critiqued by Kraabel and others), and emphasizes expressions of Jewish alienation in times of acute crisis, such as *3 Maccabees*, as though these provide evidence for a normative attitude. A strong expression of the idea that, for Diaspora Jews of the Second Temple period, 'Jewish life and experience centred on the territorial reality of the Land of Israel and Jerusalem its capital, on the Temple...and on the people living in the Land and in

Press, 1993); J. Barclay, *Jews in the Mediterranean Diaspora: From Alexander to Trajan (323 BCE–117 CE)* (Edinburgh: T. & T. Clark, 1996). On the notion of 'Judaisms', referring to the diversity of religious forms found in the evidence for the Jews of the Graeco-Roman period, see, among many other works, J. Neusner, W.S. Green and E.S. Frerichs (eds.), *Judaisms and their Messiahs* (Cambridge: Cambridge University Press, 1987).

10. A.T. Kraabel, 'The Roman Diaspora: Six Questionable Assumptions', *JJS* 33.1-2 (1982), pp. 445-64 (453-54).

11. See n. 12 below.

Jerusalem',[12] is found in Safrai's account of the relations between the Diaspora and the Land of Israel, where this perspective (which draws heavily on later Rabbinic writings) is at the heart of his discussion:

> All the literary sources, as also the inscriptions, give us to understand that the religious sentiment of Judaism and the practice of the Jewish law dominated the whole world of the Jewish Diaspora. The same applies to national sentiment and attachment to the Land of Israel... The Jews of the Diaspora regarded themselves as partners of their fellow-Jews in the homeland in their daily struggles and in all that happened in the Land of Israel... Though the Jews of the Diaspora were apparently part and parcel of Hellenistic culture and society, they regarded themselves essentially as Hebrews living abroad...[13]

In contrast, recent studies on the Jewish Diaspora increasingly emphasize the diversity of experience and attitudes of Jews in the Graeco-Roman period,[14] to the extent that it is claimed that 'Diaspora Judaisms reflect all the diversity that Judaisms anywhere else exhibit'.[15] There is a growing recognition that Jews in antiquity experienced very different social and political conditions,[16] and correspondingly engaged in their local political, social and cultural environments in many different ways.[17] Several recent studies of the Jewish communities of the Diaspora generally indicate that there is good evidence for many Jews integrating at a local level and expressing a real sense of identification with the local environment while maintaining their Jewish identity.[18] This must be considered alongside evidence for Jewish hostility towards aspects of non-Jewish culture

---

12. S. Safrai, 'Relations Between the Diaspora and the Land of Israel', in S. Safrai and M. Stern (eds.), *The Jewish People in the First Century* (Assen: Van Gorcum; Philadelphia: Fortress Press, 1974), pp. 184-215 (186).

13. Safrai, 'Relations', p. 185.

14. See the literature discussed in n. 9 above.

15. Overman, 'The Diaspora', p. 73.

16. On the varying social conditions of Jews in the Diaspora, see especially the discussion by Tcherikover in 'Prolegomena', *passim*.

17. See especially the recent work by Barclay who comments that 'We can expect to find an almost infinite variety in the ways [Jews] reacted to their variant milieux', Barclay, *Jews*, p. 3.

18. See especially Trebilco, *Jewish Communities, passim*; Barclay, *Jews, passim*; though, for a cautionary note, see M. Goodman, 'Jews and Judaism in the Mediterranean Diaspora in the Late-Roman Period: The Limitations of Evidence', *Journal of Mediterranean Studies* 4.2 (1994), pp. 208-24 (210-12).

which can express a sense of alienation in Diaspora social contexts and of solidarity with Jerusalem.[19]

There is also broad agreement on the centrality of the Jerusalem Temple for most Jews in this period, illustrated from literary sources and evidence for Diaspora pilgrimage and payment of the Temple tax.[20] The existence, however, of other Jewish temples[21] and of forms of Judaism which did not require or even rejected the Temple,[22] together with the lack of evidence for explicit Diaspora reaction to the destruction of the Temple in CE 70,[23] raise significant questions as to the importance or universal significance of the Jerusalem Temple for Jews.[24]

Diversity also characterizes the representation of the significance of the Land of Israel for Diaspora Jews in antiquity: a recent survey concludes that

19. On Jewish 'cultural antagonism', see Barclay, *Jews*, pp. 181-230; for an example of the expression of Diaspora alienation and attachment to Jerusalem, see his discussion of *3 Maccabees* (Barclay, *Jews*, pp. 198-99); see also his very useful discussion on the use of acculturation to express antagonism towards Graeco-Roman culture (Barclay, *Jews*, pp. 96-98).

20. On the significance of the Jerusalem Temple in the Second Temple Period, see E.P. Sanders, *Judaism*, Part II; C.T.R. Hayward, *The Jewish Temple* (London: Routledge, 1996). The importance of the Temple in early post-destruction Judaism is clear in works like *4 Ezra* and *2 Baruch,* which look forward to a re-established Temple; in Josephus's account of Judaism in c. 90 CE, which places the Temple cult at the centre of Jewish Law (Josephus, *Apion* 2.193-98); and in the Mishnah, which devotes much of its discussion to the subject of the maintenance of the Temple and its cult. Literary and numismatic evidence also suggests strongly that the Temple was at the centre of rebel aspirations in the Bar Kochba revolt.

21. Such as the Temple at Leontopolis in Egypt.

22. Some of the Qumran writings provide important examples of radical disaffection from the current Jerusalem Temple.

23. On the problems of the evidence, and for a suggestion linking Nerva's reform of the punitive Jewish tax imposed after 70 with Diaspora revolts under Trajan, see M. Goodman, 'Diaspora Reactions to the Destruction of the Temple', in J. Dunn (ed.), *Jews and Christians: The Parting of the Ways AD 70 to 135* (Tübingen: J.C.B. Mohr [Paul Siebeck], 1992), pp. 27-38.

24. Overman, 'The Diaspora', pp. 68-73; Barclay, *Jews*, p. 420. See also D. Schwartz, who argues that Hellenistic conceptions about the immutability of the divine made the Temple less significant for 'Hellenistic Jews', in 'Temple or City: What did Hellenistic Jews see in Jerusalem?', in Poorthuis and Safrai (eds.), *The Centrality of Jerusalem*, pp. 114-27.

> ... while for most Diaspora Jews 'the holy land' retained some religious
> significance, the strength of their attachment to Palestine as 'home' prob-
> ably varied in accordance with their social and political conditions.[25]

One could consider, in this context, the examples of *Pseudo-Aristeas*
and *3 Maccabees*, both Jewish works generally thought to originate
from Ptolemaic Egypt. Both writings express a strong sense of loyalty
towards the Ptolemaic dynasty, but they contrast strongly about the
sense of where 'home' is. While *Pseudo-Aristeas* demands reverence
for the Jerusalem Temple, and presents the land of Judaea in idealistic
terms, the author's message is nevertheless that Egyptian Jews should
remain happily in the Diaspora.[26] For the author of *3 Maccabees*,
however, life in Egypt is portrayed in terms of an alien and hostile
environment for the Jews, whose loyalties belong not only with the
ruling class of Egypt but also with the Jews of Judaea.[27] Such an
approach, which allows the literary and archaeological evidence to
speak for the differing degrees of attachment towards the Land
exhibited by the Jewish evidence, is in contrast with an older view
often found in writings addressing Jewish thought in antiquity which
assumes, as we have seen above, the normative status of the centrality
of the Land of Israel (as the true homeland) for Jews in antiquity.

Moreover, Jewish writings that may be presumed to originate in the
Diaspora in the Hellenistic and early Roman periods suggest that the
dominant political tendency among Diaspora Jews was loyalty to the
rulers of these territories, and participation in the culture and society
of their environment.[28] There is little unambiguous evidence for
Diaspora Jews having nationalistic aspirations that were centred on the
Land of Israel prior to the destruction of the Temple.[29] The case of
the First Jewish Revolt against Rome illustrates the differing loyalties

25. Barclay, *Jews*, p. 423.

26. See the treatment of *Pseudo-Aristeas* as a message to the Jews of the Ptole-
maic Empire that they should venerate the Torah and the Jerusalem Temple, but
remain in the Diaspora and be loyal to the Ptolemaic dynasty, in J. Goldstein, 'The
Message of *Aristeas to Philocrates* in the Second Century BCE, Obey the Torah,
Venerate the Temple of Jerusalem, But Speak Greek, and Put Your Hopes in the
Ptolemaic Dynasty', in M. Mor (ed.), *Eretz Israel, Israel and the Jewish Diaspora:
Mutual Relations* (London: University Press of America, 1991), pp. 1-23.

27. Barclay, *Jews*, pp. 198-201.

28. Collins, *Between Athens and Jerusalem*, pp. 60-134.

29. Though see Barclay's treatment of *3 Maccabees* and *Third Sibylline Oracle*
in Barclay, *Jews*, pp. 192-203, 218-25.

of Jews not only within Jerusalem but also in areas wider afield. A striking example is provided in the contrasting choices made by different Jews based in the Decapolis cities in the course of the revolt. These include, on the one hand, the tragic attempts of the Jews of Scythopolis to identify as 'Scythopolitans of the Jewish persuasion', and to express their local loyalty in 66 CE by siding with their Gentile neighbours against the Jewish rebels, and, on the other, the example of Simon son of Gioras from Gerasa, the son of a convert, who appears to have identified so fully with Jerusalem and the rebel cause that he took on the status of the most important Jewish rebel leader.[30]

To what extent early post-destruction aspirations for the restoration of Jerusalem, as seen in works like *4 Ezra*, represent Diaspora sentiment is difficult to determine because of our ignorance about the origins of such works. It is possible that Jewish Diaspora rebellions under Trajan in 115–17 CE may have been connected with hopes for the restoration of the Jewish State in the Land of Israel, and particularly with messianic hopes for the final return of the Jews from the Diaspora.[31] It is certainly significant that the Bar Kochba rebels' nationalist aspirations did not, as far as we know, receive support from Diaspora sources (though these would, in any case, have been considerably diminished in power if not in motivation by the bloody suppression of the Diaspora revolts under Trajan). An interesting example of Diaspora attachment to the Land of Israel in this later period is the development of the practice of transferring the remains of Diaspora Jews to the Land of Israel for reinterment there. The practice appears to have been connected with pious motives, namely the belief that the resurrection of the dead would take place first in the Land of Israel, and that burial in the Land atoned for sin.[32] The question of Jewish local patriotism in the post-destruction period has

30. M. Goodman, 'Jews in the Decapolis', *Aram* 4.1-2 (1992), pp. 49-56.

31. On 'the Messianic character of the whole movement' see Tcherikover, 'Prolegomena', pp. 90-91; for a brief critique of the messianic explanation, and for an alternative view proposing that the revolts originated in fears that Rome's conquest of Mesopotamia threatened the Jewish way of life there, see T. Barnes, 'Trajan and the Jews', *JJS* 40 (1989), pp. 145-62 (161-62).

32. I. Gafni, 'Reinterment in the Land of Israel: Notes on the Origin and Development of the Custom', in *The Jerusalem Cathedra*, I (Jerusalem: Yad Izhak Ben Zvi, 1981), pp. 96-104; E.M. Meyers, *Jewish Ossuaries: Reburial and Rebirth* (Rome: Biblical Institute Press, 1971), p. 95 and *passim*.

received special attention in the work of Isaiah Gafni on the Jewish community in Babylonia:

> The Babylonian Jews came to regard themselves as the 'purest' of the Jewish communities in terms of their pedigree, even compared with Palestine...For many Jews—at the time and subsequently—Babylonia served as the prototype of the successful Diaspora, a place where one ought to remain until the ultimate redemption and deliverance. This obviously did not sit well with the Jewish leaders in Palestine. But Babylonian local patriotism continued to thrive. By the post-talmudic era we encounter Babylonian apologists who suggest that their land is the real land of Torah, rather than Palestine.[33]

The chapters in this book explore the question of the relationship between Jewish identity and patriotism in the period between the destruction of the First Temple and the early stages of Late Antiquity (586 BCE–c. 400 CE), with particular attention to the Graeco-Roman period. Building on and expanding recent studies of Jewish communities in that time, the authors focus, in particular, on local identification with relation to land or country and the existence of local forms of patriotism. The approaches represented are interdisciplinary in nature and draw on a wide range of sources, including archaeological remains, literary material and inscriptions. Taken together the chapters contribute to the development of a comparative perspective addressing diverse social and historical contexts and different communities, including Babylonian Rabbis in Palestine, Samaritans, Jewish communities in the European Diaspora, and the perspective of particular individuals like Philo of Alexandria. For the most part, however, they are concerned with Jewish identity and patriotism in the Diaspora, or with Jewish communities in the Land of Israel who had recently returned from a situation they regarded as exile. Such a focus proves a productive one as the experience of life in the Diaspora, and the perceived state of being in exile, appear to have led to an intensification of concern with identity and patriotism. Indeed, in illustrating the role of the Land of Israel and Jerusalem as central

33. I. Gafni, 'The World of the Talmud: From the Mishnah to the Arab Conquest', in H. Shanks (ed.), *Christianity and Rabbinic Judaism* (Washington: Biblical Archaeology Society, 1992; London: SPCK, 1993), pp. 225-66 (264-65). See, in much greater detail, I. Gafni, 'Expressions and Types of "Local Patriotism" among the Jews of Sasanian Babylonia', in Shaked and Netzer (eds.), *Irano-Judaica*, II, pp. 63-71. The question of Jewish local patriotism in antiquity is the subject of a fuller study by Gafni, see n. 7 above.

metaphors in the negotiation of identity under such circumstances, the chapters in this volume reveal the pivotal position of the Land in the story of exile and return; a story which Neusner has argued consti- tutes '...that paradigmatic statement in which every Judaism, from then to now, found its structure and deep syntax of social existence'.[34]

From the outset one of the most obvious issues that emerges con- cerns the nature of patriotism and Jewish identity during antiquity. The *Oxford English Dictionary* defines patriotism as, '[t]he character or passion of a patriot; love of or zealous devotion to one's country'.[35] Country, in turn, is defined as, '[t]he territory or land of a nation; usually an independent state, or a region once independent and still distinct in race [*sic*], language, institutions or historical memories'.[36] Hence, patriotism denotes an identification with and loyalty towards a peculiar combination of territory and nation. It is not just *any* land which brings forth such emotions, but a particular place, a 'home- land', which is assumed to be integrally and inseparably bound up with the identity and very being of a specific group of people; in the case of the Jewish people, it is the Land of Israel which is usually attributed such a status.

There are, however, complicating factors in the use of such a con- cept for the purposes of historical analysis. To begin with, the concept of patriotism is bound up, in the modern world, with nationalist ide- ology and the principle that a natural relationship exists between a nation, its country/homeland and the political body in the form of an independent state. For nationalists, patriotism involves loyalty to an existing or desired state, in that the nation and its homeland are deemed to be integrally linked to such a political form. Indeed, to add to the complexity of the question of the relationship between the Jewish people and the Land of Israel, Zionist ideology is arguably a specific variant of nationalism embodying many of its essential tenets.[37]

34. J. Neusner, *Judaism and its Social Metaphors: Israel in the History of Jew- ish Thought* (Cambridge: Cambridge University Press, 1989), p. 17.

35. 'Patriotism', *OED*, II, pp. 349-50 (349).

36. 'Country', *OED*, III, pp. 1041-43 (1042).

37. See J. Boyarin, *Storm From Paradise: The Politics Of Jewish Memory* (Minneapolis: University of Minnesota Press, 1992), pp. 116-29; S. Almog, *Zion- ism and History: The Rise of a New Jewish Consciousness* (New York: St Martin's Press, 1987); S. Almog, 'People and Land in Modern Judaism', in J. Reinharz and A. Shapira (eds.), *Essential Papers on Zionism* (New York: New York University Press, 1995), pp. 46-62.

Yet, both nationalism and Zionism are modern ideologies that emerged in the eighteenth and nineteenth centuries respectively.[38] Thus, whilst anthropological and historical studies suggest that identification and affiliation with a particular place is a universal characteristic of ethnic and national identity, care must be taken not to project the ideal model of the modern nation-state back into history.[39]

The relationship between people, politics and land can take many different forms and identification with land and country can take place at multiple different levels. Consequently, many of the chapters in this book '...move away from the predominant grounding of collective identity in exclusivist territoriality'[40] and focus on local forms of patriotism that exist in diverse relationships with various political powers. For instance, Richard Coggins reminds us that both Jewish and Samaritan communities came under the control of different foreign powers, the Seleucid Empire and the Roman Empire, in the last two centuries BCE and the first century CE. Under such circumstances, Coggins argues, patriotism may have been expressed at two levels: towards one's local community and also towards the broader Empire. In his discussion of Samaritan local patriotism he provides evidence for a complex amalgamation of both local patriotic sentiment focused on Samaria and Mount Gerizim and a broader 'patriotism' towards, or at least cooperation with, the ruling Empires, in order to maintain, he argues, a degree of religious freedom. Joshua Schwartz likewise acknowledges the possibility of multiple levels of patriotism in his study of Babylonian Rabbis in Palestine during the third and fourth centuries CE. Among these different levels he includes patriotic

38. See literature referenced in n. 37. Despite its modern pedigree, traditional attachment to Zion and pleas for Jewish redemption within Judaism were important in the development of Zionist ideology. See B. Halpern, *The Idea Of the Jewish State* (Cambridge, MA: Harvard University Press, 1961), especially Chapter 4; D. Vital, *The Origins Of Zionism* (Oxford: Clarendon Press, 1975), Chapter 1.

39. See, from different perspectives, Davies, *The Territorial Dimension*, pp. 73-74; S. Jones, *The Archaeology Of Ethnicity: Constructing Identities In the Past and the Present* (London: Routledge, 1997), pp. 98-103 and 134-36; S. Schwartz, 'Language, Power and Identity In Ancient Palestine', *Past and Present* 148 (1995), pp. 3-47 (3). For an example of scholarship based upon the projection of modern notions of the nation-state and nationalism deep into the past, see M. Sicker, *Judaism, Nationalism and the Land of Israel* (Boulder, CO: Westview Press, 1992), *passim.*

40. Boyarin, *Storm from Paradise*, p. 129.

affiliation with the Roman Empire; identification with the local region, whether that be Roman Palestine or Babylonia; and what he refers to as 'local Torah patriotism', involving identification with the local rabbinical tradition. His study reveals how, at the level of the individual, these diverse expressions of patriotism might have changed and conflicted with one another in different circumstances. Similarly, in her analysis of Philo of Alexandria's writings, Sarah Pearce suggests the complex and diverse nature of Jewish forms of identification and patriotism, in this case, in Diaspora society. Not only does Philo articulate a sense of attachment to his local Egyptian environment, which he refers to as his *patris*, or 'fatherland', but he also expresses a religious and philosophical ideal in which the true 'homeland' lies in the realm of God, or virtue, which is achieved through disassociation from any particular worldly place, perhaps revealing a tension between religious and political/ethnic forms of identification with place.

The question of whether Jewish identity and patriotism in antiquity were essentially religious or ethnic in nature is, then, a related issue that arises here. On this enduring question the authors in this volume adopt a variety of positions. For instance, in her chapter on the interpretation of Jewish identity from material remains, Siân Jones argues that, although they may be different in content, ethnic and religious identities involve similar social processes. In particular, the construction of identity often involves an opposition between 'us' and 'them' which, in diverse social and historical contexts, will lead to fluid and heterogeneous expressions of the 'same' identity. Consequently, she suggests that similar modes of analysis can be applied to both kinds of identity, and that, in many instances, religious and ethnic identity are likely to have been closely intertwined, although not necessarily in a straightforward fashion. From a different point of view, which is based more on evidential rather than theoretical considerations, Coggins explores the question of the origin and political dimensions of Samaritan ethnicity alongside the religious aspects of Samaritan affiliation with Mount Gerizim. Ultimately, he concludes that religion and ethnicity were often interwoven in such a way that it is impossible to isolate one dimension from the other in the analysis of Samaritan patriotism. Indeed, all the chapters in this volume indicate the intricate connections between the religious and ethnic dimensions of Jewish (and Samaritan) identity and patriotism in antiquity. And, despite some variation, none of the positions adopted are mutually exclusive. All tend to gravitate towards W.D. Davies's conclusion that 'the agelong engagement of Judaism with The Land in religious terms indicates that ethnicity and religion…are finally inseparable'.[41]

Given the complexities of the issues at hand it is not surprising that many of the chapters at some point discuss the interpretive problems which arise from such a project. In his analysis of the use of the word 'Hebrew(s)' in Diaspora inscriptions, Graham Harvey criticizes the traditional emphasis on etymology and advocates an approach focusing on meaning. In view of the minimal contextual evidence available, however, he stresses the difficulties arising in the interpretation of patriotic sentiment from the use of the term 'Hebrew(s)'. Although the use of such a term implies a sense of origin in the Land of Israel, Harvey argues that it is more likely to have been used as a means of claiming orthodoxy and religious piety. Coggins emphasizes the difficulties arising from the use of Jewish historical sources in the analysis of Samaritan patriotism, and the importance of adopting a critical perspective concerning Jewish biases and interests in antiquity with relation to this 'splinter' group. Similarly, Lester Grabbe underlines the need to consider the various interests and biases contained within the books of Ezra and Nehemiah, and Jones advocates a more general critical stance towards the use of textual sources in the interpretation of past identities. In contrast to much existing scholarship, which tends to 'read-off' the identity of archaeological sites and objects from a historical framework, she argues that textual and material sources are likely to contain qualitatively different manifestations of identity, and that existing modes of interpretation need to be revised in order to take these differences into account. Clearly, the overriding trend is towards adopting a cautious approach to the analysis of Jewish patriotism in antiquity, one that acknowledges the difficulties that arise from many of the sources and the scarcity of these sources in themselves. Nevertheless, despite such problems, the chapters provide valuable new insights into Jewish identity and patriotism in a variety of different contexts.

One of the most pervasive points that emerges from the various studies making up this volume is the diversity of expressions of Jewish identity and patriotism that can be found during the period concerned. Jews living in the Land of Israel and the Diaspora clearly maintained a

41. Davies, *The Territorial Dimension*, p. 142.

sense of solidarity and affiliation with the Land in many circumstances, but this varied under different conditions and at different
times. Thus, as in the case of Jewish practice and belief generally,
heterogeneity and fluidity over time were some of the overriding
characteristics. As W.D. Davies has argued elsewhere:

> To define the place of Eretz Israel in Judaism requires recognition that that
> place has changed—or, more accurately, has received different emphases
> among various groups and at different times. However persistent some
> views of, and attachments to, The Land have been, and however uniform
> the testimony in the classical sources, there has not been one unchange-
> able, essential doctrine universally and uniformly recognized by the whole
> of Judaism.[42]

In the light of the studies in this volume Davies's claim is reinforced
with relation to the particular issue of patriotism. In his review of
references to the Land in Jewish inscriptions from Europe, David Noy
demonstrates that there was considerable contact between Judaea and
Jewish communities in Europe, particularly those living in Rome.
Nevertheless, this did not lead to any uniformity in naming, or in references to the Land of Israel in surviving inscriptions. Joshua
Schwartz argues that Babylonian Rabbis in Roman Palestine espoused
a particularly vehement form of local patriotism with relation to the
Palestinian Torah in their attempts to gain acceptance and promotion
within the Palestinian Rabbinical tradition. In his discussion of the
Samaritans, Coggins reveals a very different form of local patriotic
identification with Mount Gerizim, one which often competed with
Jewish expressions of identity and patriotism and also existed alongside Samaritan patriotic affiliation with the ruling Empires. Harvey
explores Diaspora patriotism and identity through an analysis of
inscriptions containing the word 'Hebrew(s)' and argues that rather
than being a straightforward representation of patriotism the term was
used by Jews and non-Jews to mark distinctions within the Jewish
community between those who, it was claimed, had preserved their
religious piety and those who had not. Meanwhile, Grabbe provides a
similar case whereby the boundaries of Jewish identity are being
marked through the definition of correct religious practice in the
Nehemiah and Ezra reforms. Whilst the boundaries of Jewish identity
in Israel were being defined in opposition to the 'nations round about',

---

42. Davies, *The Territorial Dimension*, p. 104; see also p. 142, and *passim*;
Barclay, *Jews*.

Grabbe shows that the reforms were the product of a small group of exiles who had recently returned from Babylonia, and that they were essentially concerned with the establishment of a 'pure' community in opposition to the undifferentiated mass, including many Jews, who had remained in Judah during the Babylonian Exile. Finally, Pearce illustrates that, in the context of Roman reorganization of Egyptian society and the ensuing struggles within Alexandrian society, Philo's writings reveal an attempt to negotiate (elite) Jewish interests through the production of derogatory and stereotypical representations of Egyptian identity. In this context, he identifies Judaism with Hellenism in opposition to Egyptian culture in an attempt, perhaps, to negotiate preferential treatment from Rome; but, at the same time, even as he vilifies Egypt and Egyptian society as antithetical to the values of Judaism, he expresses an identification with Alexandria as his *patris* or 'homeland'. What these studies demonstrate, then, is that not only were there diverse expressions of local identification and patriotism among various Jewish communities in antiquity, but that these expressions were actively used in the negotiation of Jewish social and political interests, and therefore thoroughly embedded in their local contexts.

Overall, the chapters in this collection illustrate that there was rarely any fixed or 'given' relationship between the Jewish people, their 'homeland' and political independence in antiquity. The contours of Jewish identity frequently changed in response to different situations, as did the forms of patriotism expressed. Equally, the very boundaries of the Land were in flux both on the ground and in the social imagination. On this issue Boyarin's comments are illuminating:

> Geography is not determinate and fixed, but is an object of social construction and contention. To a large extent, geography is a product of and a resource in the struggle of groups of peoples to attain legitimacy and power simultaneously—that is, to make and establish themselves as nations.[43]

Such processes are clearly evident in the case of Jewish identification with the Land of Israel in the Persian, Greek and Roman periods. The distinction between 'homeland' and 'Diaspora' was inevitably a fuzzy one. On the one hand, what could be considered to be Jewish territory obviously underwent considerable changes between

---

43. Boyarin, *Storm from Paradise*, p. 117.

the diverse contexts of imperialism and limited intervals of Jewish autonomy making up the period addressed in this book.[44] On the other hand, conceptions of the Land, and loyalty towards it, were constantly shifting as representations of 'pure' or 'orthodox' Judaism, and by extension Jewish identity, were created. Through such processes, whereby idealized constructions of identity and land are produced, power relations were established and contested both within Jewish communities and between Jews and non-Jews.

44. See Barclay, *Jews*, pp. 242-43.

IDENTITIES IN PRACTICE: TOWARDS AN ARCHAEOLOGICAL PERSPECTIVE ON JEWISH IDENTITY IN ANTIQUITY*

Siân Jones

> The eighties saw the passing of the notion of a normative Judaism. The tremendous diversity within and among groups understanding themselves as Jews shattered what might have remained of any notion of 'Judaism' as a monolith.[1]

As Overman and other commentators have observed, there has been something of a 'sea change' over the last decade in the modern study of Judaism and Jewish life during the Graeco-Roman period.[2] Building on earlier work, such as that of Hengel and Smallwood, this shift involved a critique, which finally demolished the idea that a normative, homogeneous Judaism persisted in Palestine during later antiquity, and its counterpart, that a Hellenized and degraded Judaism emerged amongst the supposedly isolated and beleaguered Jewish communities of the Diaspora.[3] In place of such a dichotomy between

* I am grateful to Sarah Pearce and Colin Richards for providing useful comments on this chapter, although any errors remain my own.

1. J. Overman, 'The Diaspora in the Modern Study of Ancient Judaism', in J. Overman and R. MacLennan (eds.), *Diaspora Jews and Judaism: Essays in Honor of, and in Dialogue with, A. Thomas Kraabel* (Atlanta: Scholars Press, 1992), pp. 63-78 (63).

2. See Overman, 'The Diaspora'; J. Barclay, *Jews in the Mediterranean Diaspora: From Alexander to Trajan (323 BCE–117 CE)* (Edinburgh: T. & T. Clark, 1996), pp. 4-9; M. Goodman, 'Jews and Judaism in the Mediterranean Diaspora in the late Roman Period: The Limitations of Evidence', *Journal of Mediterranean Studies* 4.2 (1994), pp. 208-24; A.T. Kraabel, 'The Roman Diaspora: Six Questionable Assumptions', *JJS* 33.1-2 (1982), pp. 445-64.

3. M. Hengel, *Judaism and Hellenism: Studies in their Encounter in Palestine during the Early Hellenistic Period* (2 vols.; London: SCM Press, 1974) and E.M. Smallwood, *The Jews under Roman Rule from Pompey to Diocletian* (Leiden: E.J. Brill, 1976). For examples of more recent critiques and the new perspective, see those mentioned in n. 2 above, and A.T. Kraabel, 'Unity and Diversity Amongst

'normative' and 'Hellenized' Judaism, between 'homeland' and 'Diaspora', a new consensus has emerged that emphasizes the diversity of Judaism and Jewish culture in both the region of Palestine and the Diaspora, and the active and productive nature of the encounter between Jewish and Hellenistic culture. This latter trend has been particularly prominent in the study of Diaspora communities, where scholars have been concerned to overcome the traditional picture of small Jewish communities either maintaining their culture and identity through an isolationist and proselytizing stance, or gradually becoming Hellenized through interaction with other groups, thus losing their distinctiveness.

Alongside new critical readings of written sources, archaeological and epigraphic evidence have played a key role in these recent developments, being used to support arguments that Judaism and Jewish culture was indeed heterogeneous in both Palestine and the Diaspora, and that Jewish communities in the Diaspora maintained their Judaism and a distinct Jewish identity, whilst simultaneously engaging with, and appropriating, aspects of Hellenistic culture.[4] However, in order to use archaeological evidence in such a way it is necessary to attribute an identity to it, to determine which aspects of the material world were produced, used and consumed by Jewish communities. The attribution of such properties to material evidence frequently involves hidden assumptions about the nature of the relationship between culture and identity. Furthermore, aside from a few diagnostic material symbols, such designations tend to depend on historical sources for information concerning where Jewish communities lived in antiquity,

Diaspora Synagogues', in L. Levine (ed.), *The Synagogue in Late Antiquity* (Philadelphia: ASOR, 1987), pp. 49-60; T. Rajak, 'The Location of Cultures in Second Temple Palestine: The Evidence of Josephus', in R. Bauckham (ed.), *The Book of Acts in its First Century Setting: Palestinian Setting* (4 vols.; Grand Rapids: Eerdmans; Carlisle: Paternoster Press, 1995), pp. 1-14; L.V. Rutgers, *The Jews in Late Ancient Rome: Evidence of Cultural Interaction in the Roman Diaspora* (Leiden: E.J. Brill, 1995); P. Trebilco, *Jewish Communities in Asia Minor* (Cambridge: Cambridge University Press, 1991).

4.   See for example, Kraabel, 'The Roman Diaspora'; T. Rajak, 'Inscription and Context: Reading the Jewish Catacombs of Rome', in J. Willem van Henten and P. Willem van der Horst (eds.), *Studies in Early Jewish Epigraphy* (Leiden: E.J. Brill, 1994), pp. 226-41; Trebilco, *Jewish Communities*; Rutgers, *The Jews*. For a cautionary note on such uses of archaeological material see Goodman, 'Jews and Judaism', *passim*.

and where particular buildings associated with them were located. In what follows I suggest that whilst recent studies drawing on material evidence are a vast improvement on traditional approaches where archaeological remains, if considered at all, were merely slotted into a pre-existing historical framework, there is still a need for further consideration of the combined use of archaeological and historical sources, particularly in the interpretation of Jewish identity. Drawing on recent work in anthropology and sociology, I argue that the material world is intricately involved in the perception and expression of group identity, but, at the same time there is no straightforward relationship between particular types of material culture and particular identities. Moreover, there are qualitative differences in the ways in which material and literary traditions are involved in processes of self-identification, and identification by others—differences which have important implications for the interpretation of group identities in the past.

First, however, it is necessary to consider the question of the nature of Jewish identity in antiquity. There has been some debate as to whether Jewish identity at this time was primarily of a religious or an ethnic character.[5] The 'old consensus', as Kraabel has pointed out, was that Jewish activities, Jewish/non-Jewish relations, and Jewish identity in antiquity are best understood in religious terms.[6] Yet increasingly Jewish identity during the Graeco-Roman period is being seen in terms of other forms of identification, including ethnic and political identity.[7] In this chapter, I intend to look at Jewish identity as a form

5. See, for instance, K. Goudriaan, 'Ethnical Strategies in Graeco-Roman Egypt', in P. Bilde, T. Engberg-Pedersen, L. Hannestad and J. Zahle (eds.), *Ethnicity in Hellenistic Egypt* (Aarhus: Aarhus University Press, 1992), pp. 74-99 (94-95), and J. Neusner, 'Was Rabbinic Judaism Really "Ethnic"?', *CBQ* 57 (1995), pp. 281-305.

6. Kraabel, 'The Roman Diaspora', pp. 454-55.

7. See, for example, Goudriaan, 'Ethnical Strategies', *passim*; Rutgers, *The Jews*, where he argues that 'Jews did not behave differently than did any other *ethnic* groups', p. 67 (my italics), and S. Schwartz, 'Language, Power and Identity in Ancient Palestine', *Past and Present* 148 (1995), pp. 3-37, where he states that 'Of all the *national, ethnic and tribal* groups living in the Mediterranean world and the Near East... *only the Jews* produced a large body of literary writing significant parts of which have survived to the present', p. 4 (my italics). Furthermore, in Bilde *et al.* (eds.), *Ethnicity in Hellenistic Egypt*, a whole chapter has been devoted to outlining recent theories of ethnic and national identity, and other chapters obviously aim to

of cultural, or ethnic, identity, by which I mean an identity that sets a group of people apart from other groups with whom they interact or coexist in terms of some distinctive criteria, which can include language, religion, history, or any other aspect of culture. Such identities involve processes of labelling and the formation of implicit and explicit contrasts between cultural traditions.[8] Although Jewish identity in antiquity may have been primarily based on religious practices and beliefs, the formation of religious-based identity involves comparable processes to those which can be observed in other culturally-based forms of group identification. Furthermore, there is evidence that the forms of identification exhibited by Jewish communities in antiquity often incorporated other cultural and political facets. Thus, to consider Jewish identity as a form of cultural identity opens up the interpretation of Jewish self-identification, and identification by others, to the possibility of other political, cultural and territorial-based constructions of identity, alongside religious ones.

The Problem: The Interplay of Text and Material Culture in the Interpretation of Jewish Identity

Throughout the history of archaeological research, material remains have been attributed to particular named past peoples, variously known as races, nations and ethnic groups. By the early twentieth century, this concern had led to the development of a particular methodology known as culture-history. This approach allowed for the description and classification of material remains in terms of particular cultural groups, and the delineation of such groups in space and time. Its basic axiom is that the repeated association of specific styles and forms of material culture—of pottery styles, house forms, ritual practices and so on—reflect past peoples or tribes. One result is that a *fixed*, one-to-one relationship is set up between these specific styles, or forms of material culture and past tribes or ethnic groups. Any changes in the

address such theories with relation to the Jewish population in Hellenistic Egypt. See, in particular, U. Østergård, 'What is Ethnic and National Identity?', in Bilde *et al.* (eds.), *Ethnicity in Hellenistic Egypt*, pp. 16-38.

    8.   In the anthropological and sociological literature these processes have been largely considered under the rubric of ethnicity, which has been redefined as a culturally based identity, rather than one based primarily on actual descent. The latter emphasis was particularly strong in nineteenth- and earlier twentieth-century conceptions of ethnicity which were not far removed from the concept of race.

material culture are taken to reflect changes in group identity—often as a result of diffusion, assimilation and/or conquest by another group.[9]

The archaeology of the region of Palestine is no exception. Archaeologists and historians have routinely identified groups, such as the Jews of the Graeco-Roman period, and the Philistines, Canaanites and Israelites of the Iron Age, on the basis of particular types of pottery, architectural styles and iconographic symbols. Furthermore, despite an emphasis on the methodological importance of using a wide range of different kinds of material culture, in practice ethnic groups in ancient Palestine, as elsewhere, have often been identified by the presence of a few specific material traits—'ethnic markers' if you like. For instance, Israelite settlements have been identified on the basis of Iron Age 'collared-rim jars' and particular types of houses known as 'pillared four-room houses'.[10] The identification of ethnic groups from material culture is generally accepted to be more problematic during the Persian and Graeco-Roman periods due to the diversity of the population in the region of Palestine, and the increasing complexity of society, alongside the development of cultures of imperialism traditionally seen in terms of Hellenization and Romanization.[11] Nevertheless, particular types of material culture, such as ritual baths and synagogues, along with particular symbols, such as the menorah, are still taken to be diagnostically Jewish—and wherever they are found sites are interpreted as 'Jewish' sites. This whole procedure, however, depends upon the assumption that a fixed, one-to-one relationship persisted between specific types of material culture and a particular ethnic identity, in this case Israelite and Jewish identity. Furthermore,

9.   For a more detailed discussion of the development of culture-history and its basic tenets see S. Jones, *The Archaeology of Ethnicity: Constructing Identities in the Past and Present* (London: Routledge, 1997), pp. 15-26, and B.G. Trigger, *A History of Archaeological Thought* (Cambridge: Cambridge University Press, 1989), Chapter 5.

10.   E. Meyers, 'Identifying Religious and Ethnic Groups through Archaeology', in *Biblical Archaeology Today: Proceedings of the Second International Conference on Biblical Archaeology* (Jerusalem: Israel Exploration Society, 1990), pp. 738-45 (739). For an example of such uses of archaeological material for the purposes of ethnic identification see A. Mazar, *The Archaeology of the Land of the Bible 10,000-586 BCE* (Cambridge: Lutterworth, 1990).

11.   For example, see Meyers, 'Identifying Religious and Ethnic Groups', pp. 740-41.

if Jewish communities are identified on the basis of such a range of fixed material traits then it also follows that Jewish culture and identity are assumed to be monolithic and homogeneous across diverse social and historical contexts. Potential variation in other aspects of the archaeological record is often ignored, and the presence of non-Jewish material on Jewish sites is either taken as evidence for other groups, or as evidence for the Hellenization of Jewish communities and a corresponding loss of Jewish culture and identity. Again, such arguments rely on the assumption that a fixed one-to-one correlation is likely to have persisted between material culture and identity, and the notion that a particular group's culture and identity is homogeneous.

In the case of the archaeology of societies with written records—that is, 'historical archaeology'—such ethnic interpretations are usually ultimately determined by historical sources, which are used to construct a narrative framework concerning the distribution and movements of particular cultural groups. Such narrative frameworks are then used as the basis for attributing ethnic labels to particular sites and the identification of ethnically diagnostic artefacts. This procedure clearly informs the identification of Israelite sites in the Iron Age and has been explicitly outlined by Mazar in a recent textbook, *The Archaeology of Israel*. Faced with the difficulty of defining a distinctively 'Israelite' material culture, he states that:

> Our departure point in this issue should be sites which according to biblical tradition were Israelite during the period of the Judges, such as Shiloh, Mizpah, Dan and Beer-sheba; settlements with similar material culture in the same region can then be defined as Israelite.[12]

A similar rationale underlies the attachment of ethnic labels to sites and objects in later periods.[13] For instance, for the most part, the

12. Mazar, *The Archaeology of the Land of the Bible*, p. 353. There is of course some controversy as to the historical validity of the biblical tradition, particularly with relation to earlier periods such as the conquest or settlement of Canaan by the Israelites. Nevertheless, for many archaeologists and historians, the biblical tradition is still used to construct a historical framework involving varying degrees of critical textual analysis.

13. For a useful discussion of the problems arising from the use of written sources as a framework in the interpretation of archaeological remains in late antiquity see R. Vale, 'Literary Sources in Archaeological Description: the Case of Galilee, Galilees and Galileans', *JSJ* 18.2 (1987), pp. 209-26.

interpretation of forum-type structures dating to the Second Temple period within Palestine as synagogues is largely dependent on references in historical sources which refer to Jewish communities living at the same locations. Whilst those structures for which a significant proportion of the original building survives—at Masada, Herodium and Gamala—all plausibly represent assembly halls, their Jewish character is not evident in and of itself. They reveal few diagnostically Jewish architectural features or symbols, except for the Gamala building, where a six-petalled rosette has been carved over the lintel of the doorway, an ornament associated with Jewish religious contexts in the pre-70 CE period. Moreover, the way in which written sources can dominate archaeological interpretation is clearly illustrated in attempts to interpret a first-century structure of indeterminate character at Capernaum as a synagogue on the basis of references to such a synagogue in the New Testament (Mk 1.21 and Lk. 7.1 and 7.5), and its location under a later synagogue.[14] Historical models have also influenced archaeological interpretation in the opposite direction, leading to the repeated identification of archaeological sites with arguably Jewish connections as non-Jewish sites, a tendency which was especially pronounced in the study of later Roman archaeological material by Christian scholars as in the case of the catacombs of Rome.[15]

Thus, in the interpretation of Jewish identity and Jewish life in the Graeco-Roman period, as in other periods and areas where contemporary written sources are available, archaeology has been the 'handmaiden' of history. Although in earlier historical studies of Jewish culture and identity in the Graeco-Roman period, archaeological evidence often played a marginal or subordinate role, more recently it has become recognized as an important adjunct in historical investigation, providing potentially independent information about aspects of

14. R. Hachlili, *Ancient Jewish Art and Archaeology in the Land of Israel* (Leiden: E.J. Brill, 1988), p. 87. For further discussion of the interpretation of these structures as pre-70 CE synagogues, see P.V.M. Flesher, 'Palestinian Synagogues Before 70 CE: A Review of the Evidence', in D. Urman and P.V.M. Flesher (eds.), *Ancient Synagogues: Historical Analysis and Archaeological Discovery* (Leiden: E.J. Brill, 1995), pp. 27-39 (34-39).

15. See Rutgers, *The Jews*, Chapter 1, for a discussion of the way in which the Jewish catacombs of Rome were consistently ignored or marginalized in historical studies that asserted the Christian character of these burial sites.

everyday life which are largely absent from historical sources.[16] Nevertheless, the use of historical sources to provide a framework for archaeological interpretation has frequently resulted in circular modes of reasoning: archaeologists draw on the representations of group identity provided by literary sources for their interpretations, whilst these same interpretations are often used to demonstrate the validity of the literary sources. Of course, both history and archaeology have 'source-critical' methods, and in some instances archaeological evidence may cast certain historical arguments into doubt by providing contradictory evidence. However, there is still a tendency in the interpretation of the archaeological material to ignore or marginalize material which, for instance, appears to be non-Jewish on a supposedly Jewish site,[17] and likewise to ignore Jewish material on what are claimed to be non-Jewish sites, as in the catacombs of Rome.

Recently, historians have adopted critical approaches to the analysis of representations of ethnic and religious identities, including Jewish identity, in literary sources.[18] In these studies the texts are not taken at face value. Rather, they are considered in terms of the social and political contexts in which they were produced, the positions and interests of the authors and the audiences, and the active role which texts may have played in the construction and negotiation of cultural identity.[19] There are, however, very few equivalent critical analyses of the attribution of cultural identity in archaeological research. With

16. For example, Trebilco, *Jewish Communities*, p. 3.

17. Rajak, 'Inscription and Context', p. 239.

18. See, for example, M. Goodman, 'Identity and Authority in Ancient Judaism', *Judaism* 39.2 (1990), pp. 192-201; Kraabel, 'The Roman Diaspora'; A.T. Kraabel, 'Synagoga Caeca: Systematic Distortion in Gentile Interpretations of Evidence for Judaism in the Early Christian period', in J. Neusner and E.S. Frerichs (eds.), *To See Ourselves as Others See Us: Christians, Jews, 'Others', in Late Antiquity* (Chico, CA: Scholars Press, 1985), pp. 219-46; T. Rajak, 'Jews and Christians as Groups in a Pagan World', in Neusner and Frerichs (eds.), *To See Ourselves as Others See Us*, pp. 247-62; Rajak, 'Inscription and Context'.

19. Kraabel, 'Synagoga Caeca', p. 241, provides a good example of this recent trend, arguing that representations of Diaspora Jews in early Christian texts are not always as they seem. Jews in these texts are often fictional characters in disputes between Christian groups. References to Jewish practices do not necessarily indicate the presence of Jews, nor do they accurately represent Jewish practices. Such representations, he argues, are not dispassionate, 'objective' representations of Jews and Judaism.

the exception of a few cautionary statements,[20] archaeological material is still attributed a particular identity in a monolithic and fixed fashion. Indeed, archaeological description is positively saturated with discourses of individual and group identity derived from literary sources. The problem is that such discursive categories are not the subject of analysis in most of the archaeological literature. Rather, they are accepted as given and constitute an a priori framework for description, classification and interpretation. As Tessa Rajak has argued:

> To determine in advance what is Jewish and what is not (or even 'probably' not) is to operate with a pre-conception of Jewish identity when our task is, precisely, to seek to define that identity.[21]

So, how should we view the relationship between literary and material evidence in the interpretation of identity? Recent theories of cultural identity provide a useful perspective on this issue.

Culture and Identity: A Complex Relationship

Over the last three decades a considerable body of research has been carried out in the human sciences which reveals that ethnic groups are not merely culture-bearing entities. That is, group identity is not a passive and straightforward reflection of a distinct culture and language. Instead, ethnicity involves the subjective construction of identity on the basis of real or assumed shared culture and/or common descent, and groups have been defined by anthropologists and sociologists on the basis of self-definition and definition by others.[22] In

20. For example, M.D. Coogan, 'Of Cults and Cultures: Reflections on the Interpretation of Archaeological Evidence', *PEQ* 119 (1987), pp. 1-8; R.S. Hess, 'Early Israel in Canaan: A Survey of Recent Evidence and Interpretations', *PEQ* 125 (1993), pp. 125-42; Meyers, 'Identifying Religious and Ethnic Groups'.

21. Rajak, 'Inscription and Context', p. 240. Whitelam makes a similar point with relation to the identification of the Israelites in Iron Age Palestine, arguing that, '[t]he debate in archaeology has not concerned the identity of the inhabitants; this was taken for granted as self-evident until recently'. See K. Whitelam, *The Invention of Ancient Israel: The Silencing of Palestinian History* (London: Routledge, 1996), p. 188.

22. For example, see the seminal work of F. Barth, 'Introduction', in F. Barth (ed.), *Ethnic Groups and Boundaries* (Boston: Little, Brown & Co., 1969), pp. 9-38 (10 and *passim*). And for reviews of subsequent research in a similar vein, see R. Cohen, 'Ethnicity: Problem and Focus in Anthropology', *Annual Review of*

many instances, only certain cultural practices are involved in the perception and expression of ethnic difference, whilst other cultural practices and beliefs are shared across ethnic boundaries. Furthermore, the processes involved in the construction of ethnic identities and the selection of particular cultural and linguistic characteristics as relevant symbols of identity take place in the context of social interaction, and involve the ascription of identity vis-à-vis others. In many instances, this active construction of identity is embedded in the negotiation of economic and political interests, or what can be broadly termed 'power relations'. For instance, it has been shown that individuals may shift identity in different situations, or even permanently, depending on their interests,[23] and many studies have explored the ways in which ethnic groups have been formed in the context of resistance to imperial or state domination.[24]

Such processes of identity construction are clearly evident amongst Diaspora Jewish communities in the Graeco-Roman period. Recent historical studies have shown that Jewish communities in the Diaspora and in Palestine were far from homogeneous in culture or identity. The cultural practices in which Jewish communities were engaged and the nature of their interaction with non-Jewish groups varied considerably in different areas of the Graeco-Roman world and over time. For instance, in his study of Asia Minor, Trebilco has shown that even within a relatively restricted area, the lifestyles of Jewish communities living in different cities appear to have been quite diverse in terms of wealth, power and status, as manifested in inscriptions and material display.[25] Similarly, Barclay has demonstrated that Egyptian Jews of the Graeco-Roman period lived under diverse conditions and responded to those conditions in varying ways.[26] Moreover, Jewish culture and identity was continually shifting in response to new social and

Anthropology 7 (1978), pp. 379-403; T.H. Eriksen, *Ethnicity and Nationalism: Anthropological Perspectives* (London: Pluto Press); Jones, *The Archaeology of Ethnicity*, Chapters 3 and 4.

23. See, for example, Barth, 'Introduction'; H. Eidheim, 'When Ethnic Identity is a Social Stigma', in Barth (ed.) *Ethnic Groups*, pp. 39-57; E.E. Roosens, *Creating Ethnicity: The Process of Ethnogenesis* (London: Sage, 1989).

24. See J. Comaroff and J. Comaroff, *Ethnography and the Historical Imagination* (Boulder, CO: Westview Press, 1992); S.B.C. Devalle, *Discourses of Ethnicity: Culture and Protest in Jharkhand* (London: Sage, 1992).

25. Trebilco, *Jewish Communities*, Chapter 2.

26. Barclay, *Jews*, Part I.

historical contexts, such as those resulting from the Roman annexation and re-organization of Egypt by Octavian in 30 BCE, or the imposition of the *fiscus Judaicus* after 70 CE by the Emperor Vespasian.[27] Indeed, such situations, in demanding self-conscious articulations of Jewish identity, reveal the way in which 'Jewishness' was often constructed in opposition to 'others', such as the Egyptians.[28] And, furthermore, it is in such contexts that the intersection between power and identity is highlighted as new representations of Jewishness were constructed by both Jews and non-Jews in the negotiation of economic and political relations, and the right to some degree of selfdetermination in cultural and religious spheres.[29]

Such developments in our understanding of group identity in general, and Jewish identity in particular, have important implications for the interpretation of identity from archaeological remains. As recent studies challenge the traditional notion of ethnic groups as culture-bearing units, it can no longer be assumed, as in culture-historical archaeology, that archaeological culture groups reflect past peoples.[30] A particular group's identity is unlikely to be monolithic or homogeneous, and the same is true for the cultural beliefs and practices which inform that identity. Thus, we would be unlikely to find a particular ethnic or religious group represented by a discrete, uniform pattern of particular types of material culture in the archaeological record. Furthermore, it cannot be assumed that there is a fixed relationship between particular types of material culture and a particular identity. The types of material associated with a particular group's identity may change in different situations and through time. Consequently, we

27. On Egypt, see Barclay, *Jews*; Goudriaan, 'Ethnical Strategies'; on the *fiscus Judaicus* see Goodman, 'Identity and Authority'.

28. See the chapter by S. Pearce in this volume.

29. See, for example, Goudriaan, 'Ethnical Strategies', *passim*.

30. This point has been stressed from a variety of positions from the 1960s onwards. For examples see L.R. Binford, 'Archaeology as Anthropology', *American Antiquity* 28 (1962), pp. 217-25 (219); P.J. Ucko, 'Ethnography and the Archaeological Interpretation of Funerary Remains', *World Archaeology* 1.2 (1969), pp. 262-80; I. Hodder, 'Simple Correlations Between Material Culture and Society', in I. Hodder (ed.), *The Spatial Organization of Culture* (London: Gerald Duckworth, 1978), pp. 3-24; C. Renfrew, *Archaeology and Language: The Puzzle of Indo-European Origins* (London: Penguin Books, 1987); S.J. Shennan, 'Introduction', in S.J. Shennan (ed.), *Archaeological Approaches to Cultural Identity* (London: Unwin & Hyman, 1989), pp. 1-32.

cannot take it for granted that particular types of material culture represent a particular group of people across space and time, nor can we assume that changes in material culture which have been seen as evidence for acculturation represent a straightforward change in, or loss of, identity. Rather, particular material culture styles may have been deliberately appropriated and redefined in the expression of group identity.

Nevertheless, with a few important exceptions, these implications have been largely ignored in the attribution of Jewish identity to archaeological remains in antiquity. In some instances, the response has been one of extreme caution or scepticism, but, in many cases, material evidence is still regarded as a direct reflection of group identity. So, for instance, buildings of some size and wealth displaying symbols conventionally associated with the Jews, such as the synagogue at Sardis, are taken as evidence for a thriving Jewish community with a strong sense of its own culture and identity. This may well have been the case, but such arguments still rely on questionable attributions of identity to particular styles of material culture in a uniform and fixed fashion. Instead, we need to consider the way in which identities are continuously constructed through the material world as objects are produced and used in different contexts associated with different social practices. For instance, in recent studies of the menorah as a symbol it has been argued that its early use on ossuaries and oil lamps was restricted to contexts which were religious in nature and probably associated with a priestly class.[31] Later on, mostly in the Diaspora, the menorah symbol was used in broader contexts where it was represented in the form of decoration or graffiti adorning buildings, or accompanying inscriptions. It has also been argued that such uses of the menorah image disregarded contemporary religious prohibitions on its representation and were likely to have had a wider meaning.[32] Here, then, we may be looking at a situation where the meaning of a particular symbol changed in different situations. In the first instance, the context in which it was used suggests that its

31. For detailed discussions on the history of visual representations of the menorah, see R. Hachlili, *Ancient Jewish Art and Archaeology in the Land of Israel* (Leiden: E.J. Brill, 1988) and L.Y. Rahmani, 'Representations of the Menorah on Ossuaries', in H. Geva (ed.), *Ancient Jerusalem Revealed* (Jerusalem: Israel Exploration Society, 1994), pp. 239-43.

32. Hachlili, *Ancient Jewish Art*, p. 253.

significance was limited to the religious domain within the Jewish community. But later on the image may have been appropriated in the communication of 'Jewishness' in opposition to other groups of people, a need which is likely to have been particularly acute in the Diaspora where such representations of the menorah appear to originate.[33] This type of analysis allows us to move away from straightforward ethnic labelling of sites and material, that is menorah = Jewish symbol = Jewish site. By following the social history of particular objects and symbols through changing contexts, we can start to look at how identities were constructed through material culture in opposition to other groups, and how the expression of identity may have changed over time.

Much of the archaeological evidence relating to Jewish communities of the Graeco-Roman period suggests that in the context of imperial rule and the encounter with Hellenistic culture, Jewish identity persisted, and that the adoption of Hellenistic culture may well have represented the deliberate appropriation and redefinition of, say, pagan material culture in a Jewish context.[34] But at the same time there was clearly a diverse range of responses in terms of the kinds of material culture which were being produced and consumed by Jewish communities. Given that there was likely to have been a dynamic relationship between particular types of material culture and the expression of identity, it is difficult to ascertain which aspects of material culture were involved in the expression of Jewish identity. So how should we approach the relationship between material culture and identity if it is not a fixed and intrinsic one? This question inevitably touches on the issue of the relationship between people's perceptions of cultural identity and the cultural practices and social relations in which they engage; or, to put it in a more general way, the

33. Hachlili, *Ancient Jewish Art*, p. 254, and Rahmani, 'Representations of the Menorah', p. 243. The use of the Menorah on a coin of the last Hasmonean king, Mattathias Antigonus, may provide an earlier example of its use as a symbol of Jewishness during the first century BCE. The menorah may have been used in this context to stress Antigonus' priestly status and/or Jewishness as a means of legitimating his political power. See Hachlili, *Ancient Jewish Art*, p. 238.

34. For instance, Rajak argues that the use of sarcophogi in the Jewish catacombs of Rome, and particularly the Jewish 'seasons' sarcophagus where the menorah replaces the usual portrait in the central roundel, represents the appropriation of non-Jewish material culture in the expression of Jewish identity. See Rajak 'Inscription and Context', p. 235.

relationship between people's theory and their practice. This issue is obviously of crucial importance for archaeologists if we are to analyse cultural identity from the material remains of past societies, as we do not have direct access to people's beliefs and ideas. It is also central to the development of a critical approach to the relationship between the archaeological material and the various cultural identities referred to in historical sources.

A Practice Theory of Ethnicity

The relationship between people's consciousness of ethnicity and their cultural contexts can be explored through theories of practice that address the general relationship between the conditions of social life and people's subjective constructions of social reality.[35] The anthropologist Pierre Bourdieu has argued that people possess durable, often subliminal, dispositions towards certain perceptions and practices (such as those relating to the sexual division of labour, morality, tastes and so on).[36] Such dispositions become part of an individual's sense of self at an early age, and are generated by the conditions making up a particular social environment, such as modes of production or access to certain resources.[37] Bourdieu calls the totality of these dispositions 'the habitus'. In contrast to traditional theories of culture, the habitus does not consist of a system of normative rules that exist outside of individual history.[38] Rather, the orientations of the habitus 'are at once "structuring structures" and "structured structures"; they shape and are shaped by social practice'.[39]

The concept of the habitus can be used to explain the way in which subjective ethnic classifications are grounded in the social conditions characterizing particular social domains. Ethnicity is not a passive reflection of similarities and differences in the cultural practices and structural conditions in which agents are socialized. Nor is ethnicity

35. See G.C. Bentley, 'Ethnicity and Practice', *Comparative Studies in Society and History* 29 (1987), pp. 24-55, and Jones, *The Archaeology of Ethnicity*.

36. P. Bourdieu, *Outline of a Theory of Practice* (Cambridge: Cambridge University Press, 1977), p. 72.

37. Bourdieu, *Outline*, pp. 77-93.

38. Bourdieu, *Outline*, p. 72.

39. M. Postone, E. LiPuma and C. Calhoun, 'Introduction: Bourdieu and Social Theory', in C. Calhoun, E. LiPuma and M. Postone (eds.), *Bourdieu: Critical Perspectives* (Cambridge: Polity Press, 1993), p. 4.

entirely constituted in the process of social interaction, whereby cultural characteristics are manipulated in the pursuit of economic and political interests. Rather, drawing on Bourdieu's theory of practice, it can be argued that the construction of ethnic identity is grounded in the shared subliminal dispositions of the habitus which shape, and are shaped, by commonalities of practice:

> [a] shared habitus engenders feelings of identification among people similarly endowed. Those feelings are consciously appropriated and given form through existing symbolic resources.[40]

Furthermore, these 'symbolic resources', such as language, material culture, beliefs and so on, are not arbitrary. The cultural practices and beliefs which become reified as symbols of ethnicity are derived from, and resonate with, people's habitual practices and experiences, as well as reflecting the immediate conditions and interests that characterize particular situations. As Eriksen has argued, symbols of ethnicity

> ... are intrinsically linked with experienced, practical worlds containing specific, relevant meanings which on the one hand contribute to shaping interaction, and on the other hand limit the number of options in the production of ethnic signs.[41]

Yet the habitus and ethnicity are not directly congruent, as in the traditional equation of culture and ethnicity. There is a break between the cultural dispositions making up the habitus as a whole, and the objectified representation of cultural difference involved in the expression of ethnicity. Shared habitual dispositions provide the basis for the recognition of commonalities of sentiment and interest and the perception and communication of cultural affinities and differences that ethnicity entails. However, a consciousness of ethnicity only emerges in the context of social interaction between people of differing cultural traditions. Such forms of interaction lead to a reflexive mode of perception involving a conscious rationalization of cultural practices which had previously constituted subliminal, taken-for-granted modes of behaviour. Such exposure to the arbitrariness of cultural practices, which had hitherto been taken been taken as self-evident and natural, permits and requires a change 'in the level of

---

40. Bentley, 'Ethnicity and Practice', p. 173.

41. T.H. Eriksen, *Us and Them in Modern Societies: Ethnicity and Nationalism in Mauritius, Trinidad and Beyond* (London: Scandinavian University Press, 1992), p. 45.

discourse, so as to rationalize and systematize' the representation of those cultural practices, and, more generally, the representation of the cultural tradition itself.[42] It is at such a discursive level that ethnic categories are produced, reproduced and transformed through the systematic communication of cultural difference with relation to particular 'ethnic others'.[43]

Thus, the form which expressions of cultural difference take is a product of the intersection of people's habitus with the social conditions constituting a particular historical context. These conditions include the prevailing modes of domination, and the relative distribution of the material and symbolic means necessary for the imposition of dominant regimes of ethnic categorization. Hence, the extent to which ethnicity is embedded in pre-existing cultural realities represented by a shared habitus is highly variable and contingent upon the cultural transformations engendered by the processes of interaction and the nature of the power relations between the interacting 'groups'.[44] Moreover, expressions of ethnic difference are a product of the interrelation between the particular cultural practices and historical experiences activated in any given social context, and broader discourses of ethnicity. Consequently, the cultural content of ethnicity may vary substantively and qualitatively in different contexts, as may the importance of ethnicity.[45]

42. Bourdieu, *Outline*, p. 233.

43. There are numerous examples of this process in the ethnographic literature. For instance, in the process of interaction and communication between the Tswana people of southern Africa and evangelist missionaries, both groups began to recognize distinctions between them. In effect they began to objectify their world in relation to a novel other, and in the process they invented for themselves a self-conscious coherence and distinctness. This objectification of culture is not a fabrication, an entirely instrumental construction. Tswana ethnicity is based on the perception of commonalities of practice and experience in Setswana (Tswana ways) in opposition to Sekgoa (European ways). But it has also been fundamentally affected by the colonial situation, which resulted in a break with pre-existing forms of identity. It was only as a result of the interaction between the Tswana and members of the colonial society that Tswana tradition was objectified as a coherent body of knowledge and practice uniting the Tswana people as an ethnic group. For further discussion see Comaroff and Comaroff, *Ethnography and the Historical Imagination*.

44. Comaroff and Comaroff, *Ethnography and the Historical Imagination*, p. 56.

45. See Eriksen, *Us and Them*, p. 33 and *passim*.

Such a theory accounts for the dynamic and contextual nature of ethnicity at the same time as addressing the relationship between people's perceptions of ethnicity, and the cultural practices and social relations in which they are embedded. Furthermore, it suggests that there are likely to be significant differences between discursive literary representations of ethnicity and its manifestation in social practice which have important implications for the interpretation of ethnic groups in historical archaeology.

Practice and Representation

The theory of ethnicity proposed here suggests that archaeologists may not be able to find a reflection of the 'ethnic entities' represented in historical sources in the archaeological record. Indeed, it is possible to question the very existence of bounded, homogeneous ethnic entities except at an abstract conceptual level. Ethnic categories are based on a conscious reification of transient cultural practices taking place in different spatial and temporal contexts,[46] and the 'group' only exists in the context of interpretation where it justifies and explains past practices and modes of interaction and informs future ones. In contrast, the praxis of ethnicity results in multiple transient realizations of ethnic difference in particular contexts. These practical realizations of ethnicity, in many instances, involve the repeated production and consumption of distinctive styles of material culture. Nevertheless, they are a product of the intersection of the perceptual and practical dispositions of the people concerned and the interests and oppositions engendered in a particular social context, rather than abstract categories of difference.

This distinction between abstract conceptual representations of ethnicity and the praxis of ethnicity is, in some senses, analogous to the anthropologist, Paul Connerton's distinction between contexts of 'inscription' and 'incorporation'.[47] Abstract representations of ethnicity are frequently found in 'inscribing practices', such as writing, art, and other symbolic forms, that trap and hold information long after the 'author' has stopped informing. Whereas, in contrast, the praxis of

46. Cf. P. Bourdieu, *The Logic of Practice* (Cambridge: Polity Press, 1990), p. 84, on genealogy and mapping.

47. P. Connerton, *How Societies Remember* (Cambridge: Cambridge University Press, 1989), p. 72-73.

ethnicity falls in the domain of 'incorporating practice', such as everyday practices, performative acts, and bodily comportment, which carry messages that a sender or senders 'impart by means of their current bodily activity, the transmission occurring only during the time that their bodies are present to sustain that activity'.[48]

These different forms of practice, inscriptive and incorporating, should not be seen as exclusive, fixed categories, as they overlap with one another and persist alongside one another in any particular socio-historical situation. But they represent a useful heuristic device in that they allow us to isolate qualitative differences in the manifestation of ethnicity in different contexts. As Connerton points out, interpretive history has traditionally taken inscription, most commonly textual inscription, as its privileged object of enquiry.[49] In reconstructing past ethnic groups, historians and archaeologists have colluded in giving precedence to literary representations of ethnicity and searching for an isomorphic reflection of such categories in the archaeological record. Yet to do so, I suggest, is to make the mistake of conflating qualitatively different manifestations of ethnicity. The archaeological record may provide evidence for some aspects of inscriptive practice—as in the case of symbolic motifs, such as the menorah image, which become objectifed as representations of a particular group's identity. The vast proportion of the material recovered by archaeologists is, however, likely to be the product of transient, but ongoing, cultural practices, some of which may have been involved in the recognition and expression of ethnic difference.

This is not to suggest that the majority of archaeological material is not relevant to the analysis of ethnicity. On the contrary, the analysis of such material can provide important information about the experienced, practical contexts with which inscriptive representations, or discourses, of group identity intersect, and from which they derive their power. Consequently, I suggest that we need to focus on the social practices which would have been associated with particular material forms and structures, rather than their stylistic history. For instance, in analyzing ancient synagogues of the Roman and Byzantine periods, archaeologists have focused on architectural history with the aim of elucidating origins and identifying diagnostic features. An alternative way of approaching such sites would be to focus on the

48. Connerton, *How Societies Remember*, p. 72
49. Connerton, *How Societies Remember*, pp. 4, 100-101.

social practices involved in the use of the synagogue and how its material form would have structured those practices.[50] If, as I have argued above, group identities are often founded upon everyday practices and the material domains associated with them, then it seems likely that the broad communal participation and variety of practices associated with the synagogue in antiquity would have resulted in different manifestations of Judaism and Jewish identity from those associated with the Temple cult. That is not to suggest that, for instance, Jews living in the Diaspora, practising their religion in the context of local synagogues, would have developed an alternative group identity from those, say, living in Jerusalem prior to 70 CE, but that they may have seen and expressed their Jewishness in different ways as a result of the social practices and material domains which they experienced.

Such an emphasis on the material domains in which identities are formed would provide a useful complement to recent historical studies, as material culture potentially provides access to multivocal practices, which can be reduced to the decontextualized, univocal, representations by using certain forms of textual analysis. The point that I wish to emphasize here is the importance of recognizing the qualitative difference between objectified, inscriptive, representations of ethnicity and the praxis of ethnicity. Rather than the seemingly coherent ethnic categories which are produced at a discursive level, the praxis of ethnicity may be manifested in the archaeological record as a complex web of overlapping stylistic boundaries constituted by expressions of ethnic difference, expressions which were at once transient, but also subject to reproduction and transformation in the ongoing processes of social life.

Conclusion

This chapter represents preliminary work, and it is not based on a substantive reanalysis of the archaeological material relating to Jewish communities of the Graeco-Roman period. Nevertheless, the theory of ethnicity discussed has important implications for the conventional use of literary representations of Jewish identity as a framework for the

50. For a recent historical study focusing on the social aspects and implications of early synagogues and their appearance in ancient Palestine see Flesher, 'Palestinian Synagogues'.

interpretation of the archaeological evidence. Furthermore, it suggests some fruitful directions for the use of archaeological evidence in the interpretation of Jewish self-identification in the Graeco-Roman period.

Material culture and literature may be intertwined in common representations of cultural identity. I have argued, however, that there are important qualitative differences between the representation of cultural identity in literature, and the expressions of identity embodied in the cultural practices which have contributed to much of the archaeological record. Thus, it cannot be assumed that discursive, literary representations of Jewish identity will be directly reflected in the archaeological evidence. Nevertheless, if Jewish identity is not assumed to be monolithic, and a distinction between people's ideas or beliefs and their practices is accepted, then in practice there is potential for the analysis of multiple, contextual expressions of Jewish identity based on archaeological material. In engaging with such a project archaeologists may be able to explore the ways in which discursive systems of difference intersect with the values and modes of practice characterizing particular contexts. At present, very few historians or archaeologists recognize the potential of archaeology in this area. Yet a contextual and meaning-centred approach to the archaeological analysis of cultural identity offers an appropriate counterpart to recent critical studies of representations of Jewish identity in the historical sources.

Future archaeological research based on these kinds of approaches could, I believe, contribute to recent work challenging traditional oppositions, such as Hellenism and Judaism, and their interpretation in terms of discrete, coherent cultural and ethnic entities. Instead of two incompatible and fixed systems a more diverse and heterogeneous picture is likely to emerge in which Greek and Jewish cultural forms were closely intertwined. Aspects of both Greek and Jewish culture may have been appropriated by different communities within the eastern Mediterranean in the expression of diverse identities in changing situations. As Tessa Rajak has pointed out, the dichotomy between Hellenism and Judaism may itself be a product of particular moments of identity construction when 'the Jews saw themselves as diametrically opposed to what the Greeks stood for in the broadest sense' and a sharp polarization manifested itself, often leading to conflict.[51] But, as

51. Rajak, 'The Location of Cultures', p. 4.

she herself stresses, these are likely to have been rare historical moments, and such categories probably had little importance in terms of day-to-day interactions.[52] They thus provide an example of the relational and symbolic character of discursive representations of group identity, which in practice may have been manifested in multiple, overlapping, and heterogeneous forms.

52. Rajak, 'The Location of Cultures', p. 5.

TRIUMPH OF THE PIOUS OR FAILURE OF THE XENOPHOBES? THE EZRA–NEHEMIAH REFORMS AND THEIR *NACHGESCHICHTE*

Lester L. Grabbe

A major bias throughout much of the biblical text is the polarity of faithfulness to Yahweh versus falling away into disobedience or false worship. The text works on the assumption that God delivered a religion pure and undefiled to Israel at the beginning but that Israel continually went astray from that strait and narrow path. Furthermore, Israel is perpetually warned against the dangers from the nations roundabout: watch out for Johnny foreigner because he—or especially she—will lead you away from proper worship into paganism, idolatry, and utter depravity.

In the Hebrew Bible this attitude reaches its climax in the books of Ezra and Nehemiah in which many of the people, even some of the priests, have contracted marriages with foreign wives and are required to separate from their families. Many modern treatments accept the bias of the text at face value. What Ezra and Nehemiah did was a Good Thing, to be highly commended. Their reforms are a model of piety, proper religion, and godly conduct.

The attitudes and perspectives exemplified in the Ezra–Nehemiah reforms, if not the reforms themselves, became an important part of the later religious identity of the Jews. Perhaps this is one of the reasons that modern scholars have been so ready to accept the judgment of the text; hermeneutical concerns have influenced historical assessment. This paper intends to look beyond the bias of the text and ask to what extent the reforms of Ezra–Nehemiah were popular and how long they lasted.

The reforms included a variety of elements. The main two are: (1) a strict enforcement of religious law; and (2) a cutting of all ties (marriage, business, etc.) with the 'peoples of the lands'/'foreigners'. The first of these is readily understandable and, even though it is not entirely divorced from the second, it is not the main issue and will not be discussed further. My principal concern is the second: the building of barriers against 'foreigners'. To what extent was this acceptable to all Jews, and how viable was it as a policy? An evaluation of these reforms can best be appreciated by seeing how matters in Judah fared for the next few centuries.

The Reforms of Ezra and Nehemiah

The Problem of Sources

Ezra and Nehemiah are often treated as a unit that outlines the history of the Jews in the land in the first part of the Persian period. A number of recent studies have become much more sceptical about the amount of factual history in the two books, though there is no general agreement. If there is any sort of consensus, it is that an actual account of Nehemiah (a Nehemiah 'Memorial' or 'Memoir') lies behind much of the book of Nehemiah. The task of sorting out the boundaries of this Memorial and discerning how thoroughly it has been edited still requires much work, but a valuable contemporary original source seems to shine through a good portion of the text.[1]

The situation is different with regard to Ezra.[2] The sources of information for the book are less certain. The Ezra of the book is himself a shadowy figure who seems to recede from us as we try to look more closely at him.[3] Some have even doubted that he existed at all.[4] On the other hand, it has long been speculated that an 'Ezra

1. Recent studies accepting this point of view are H.G.M. Williamson, *Ezra, Nehemiah* (WBC, 16; Waco, TX: Word Books, 1985); A.H.J. Gunneweg, *Nehemiah* (KAT, 19.2; Gütersloh: Gerd Mohn, 1987); J. Blenkinsopp, *Ezra–Nehemiah* (OTL; London: SCM Press, 1989).

2. See L.L. Grabbe, 'Reconstructing History from the Book of Ezra', in P.R. Davies (ed.), *Studies in the Second Temple* (JSOTSup, 117; Sheffield: Sheffield Academic Press, 1991), pp. 98-106; A.H.J. Gunneweg, *Esra* (KAT, 19.1; Gütersloh: Gerd Mohn, 1985).

3. See especially L.L. Grabbe, 'What Was Ezra's Mission?', in T.C. Eskenazi and K.H. Richards (eds.), *Second Temple Studies. II. Temple Community in the Persian Period* (JSOTSup, 175; Sheffield: Sheffield Academic Press, 1994), pp. 286-99.

4. C.C. Torrey, *The Composition and Historical Value of Ezra–Nehemiah* (BZAW, 2; Giessen: Ricker, 1896); G. Garbini, *History and Ideology in Ancient Israel* (London: SCM Press, 1988), pp. 151-69.

Memoir' lies behind Ezra 7–10.[5] If so, it has been so extensively edited and supplemented that the historical figure can be glimpsed only dimly, if at all. The problematic nature of the sources applies to the reforms as well. According to the text, the problem of mixed marriages was raised in a similar fashion during the time of both Ezra and Nehemiah. Although it is not impossible that the same problem arose on two separate occasions, the failure of Nehemiah to refer to Ezra's reforms or vice versa cannot but make one suspicious that one is modelled on the other, that is, that one is a literary creation based on the other.[6]

There is also the relationship between the passages describing the reforms in Ezra and Nehemiah. Nehemiah 8 has conventionally been associated with Ezra 7–10. Nehemiah 9–10 also seem to be related to the Ezra story in some way, though they are probably separate from Nehemiah 8.[7] The relationship of Nehemiah 9 to Nehemiah 10 is also a puzzle: although on the surface it appears to continue the question of 'foreign' marriages, it is actually only vaguely related. Furthermore, many have been suspicious of the list of signatories.[8] A parallel between it and the content of Nehemiah 13 has also been noted, which could suggest that the former has been modelled on the latter. It is not surprising, therefore, that the order and relationship between the various passages describing the reforms have been the subject of considerable debate; whatever conclusions one comes to will very much affect the question of historicity.

The historical question is thus a difficult one, but it need not be resolved here. I think the existence of a reform of some kind is

5.   See L.W. Batten, *A Critical and Exegetical Commentary on Ezra and Nehemiah* (ICC; Edinburgh: T. & T. Clark, 1913); W. Rudolph, *Esra und Nehemia* (HAT, 20; Tübingen: J.C.B. Mohr [Paul Siebeck], 1949); Williamson, *Ezra, Nehemiah*, pp. xxviii-xxxii, who gives a useful survey of scholarship on the question.

6.   This is indeed the argument of Gunneweg, *Esra*, p. 163, who concludes that Ezra's reform is based on Neh. 13.23-28.

7.   Cf. the survey in Williamson, *Ezra, Nehemiah*, pp. 273-74.

8.   S. Mowinckel, *Studien zu dem Buche Ezra–Nehemiah* (Skrifter utgitt av Det Norske Videnskaps-Akademi i Oslo, II; Hist.-Filos. Klasse. Ny Serie, 3; Oslo: Universitetsforlaget, 1964), I, pp. 134-45, argued that the signature list was an artificial creation by the editor of Nehemiah. In this he is more or less followed by Blenkinsopp, *Ezra–Nehemiah*, pp. 311-14; Williamson, *Ezra, Nehemiah*, pp. 328-31; and Gunneweg, *Nehemia*, pp. 133-34.

sufficiently well attested to proceed on that basis. Whether there was one or two or even more acts of mandatory divorce followed by repentance is immaterial for my purposes. The basic reforms are accepted, but it is difficult to have too much confidence in the details. At this point it is necessary to see what the accounts actually say.

The Reforms
According to Ezra 9–10, it was the leaders of the community who reported to Ezra that the people had intermarried with the 'peoples of the land(s)' (on this term, see below). Surprisingly, Ezra himself took no direct action at this point but instead tore his clothes and hair, fasted, and prayed for forgiveness. The people seemed to gather to him of their own accord. A decree followed (sent by whom?) for all the people to assemble in Jerusalem. When they did, Ezra finally summoned up some initiative of his own and called on the people to separate from the 'peoples of the lands' and from their 'foreign' wives (9.1, 2; 10.2, 10, 14, 17, 18, 44). In setting up the procedure for resolving the problem, Ezra also seems to have taken the lead even though it was a collective action by the Jerusalem leadership. The book concludes with a list of those who had transgressed the covenant, including priests and Levites as well as normal Israelites.

Of particular interest in interpreting this passage is the reference to 'those who tremble' (כל חרד Ezra 9.4; החרדים Ezra 10.3) at God's word. It has been argued that this is a reference to a religious party with a specific outlook and programme, a party known also from references in Isaiah 57, 65, and 66.[9] This does not by itself prove the historicity of the Ezra account since the hypothesis of the החרדים must be established on other grounds. However, if this thesis is correct, Ezra would have been supported by only a narrow power base, not by the majority of the people.

I now move to Nehemiah. If a contemporary original source from Nehemiah himself indeed lies behind the book preserved in his name, we still have to deal with the bias of that account. Nehemiah seems to have been a man of strong convictions and few doubts about his own rightness in all his actions. Therefore, he gives his account from a very personal and particular viewpoint and makes no pretense of

---

9. Blenkinsopp, *Ezra–Nehemiah*, pp. 178-79; J. Blenkinsopp, 'A Jewish Sect of the Persian Period', *CBQ* 52 (1990), pp. 5-20.

trying to be evenhanded or fair to his opponents.[10] It is clear that he was a zealot for what he understood to be God's will.

Nehemiah's initial task was to rebuild the wall around Jerusalem. He anticipated trouble from the beginning because his first reconnaissance of the task was done secretly at night—without telling any of the Jerusalem officials (Neh. 2.11-16). Why was this? No explanation is given. What we do see is that despite the general acquiescence to Nehemiah's various demands, there was strong opposition to Nehemiah in some quarters, nor was this opposition solely from outsiders.

Opposition to the wall seems initially to have come only from those outside Jerusalem: Sanballat who was governor of Samaria, Geshem the Arab, and Tobiah, labelled an 'Ammonite slave', but evidently from an old Jewish family of the Transjordanian region.[11] In spite of Nehemiah's evident mistrust of his colleagues, the people of Jerusalem appear to have buckled down to the task of building the wall without any evidence of dissent (Neh. 3), at least at first. However, even before the wall was finished there is a suggestion that some were against Nehemiah (see below).

The passage in Nehemiah describing the separation from the 'sons of the foreigner' (Neh 9.2: בני נכר) is comprised of chs. 8–10. It is widely accepted that this is not a part of the Nehemiah Memorial. Nehemiah himself does not appear in the account except in two verses. In Neh. 8.9 the reference to Nehemiah is likely to be a secondary addition.[12] Nehemiah 10.2 lists Nehemiah's name at the head of those who signed the pledge to separate from 'peoples of the land', though this list seems to come from a source separate from chs. 8–9. A further indication that this section is an insertion into the Nehemiah Memoir is found in Neh 13.1-3 (a part of the Nehemiah Memoir),

10. Cf. David J.A. Clines, 'The Nehemiah Memoir: The Perils of Autobiography', in *What Does Eve Do to Help? and Other Readerly Questions to the Old Testament* (JSOTSup, 94; Sheffield: Sheffield Academic Press, 1990), pp. 124-64.

11. The term העבד could designate anything from a royal officer ('servant' of the king) to the lowest slave. One suspects that Nehemiah is using it ironically, however, because he also designates Tobiah as 'Ammonite', even though he is most likely Jewish, and Sanballat as 'the Horonite', even though he held the important office of Persian provincial governor. The evidence for Tobiah's origins are given in B. Mazar, 'The Tobiads', *IEJ* 7 (1957), pp. 137-45, 229-38; revision of articles in *Tarbiz* 12 (1941), pp. 109-23, and *Eretz-Israel* 4 (1956), pp. 249-51.

12. E.g. Williamson, *Ezra, Nehemiah*, p. 279.

which speaks of separating the 'mixture' from Israel as if knowing nothing about the events described in chs. 8–10.

Almost no opposition to the separation from their wives is recorded in either Ezra (except possibly for two individuals in 10.15) or Nehemiah. But a close reading of the text does show a good deal of opposition to Nehemiah from within the Jerusalem community. According to Nehemiah, Shemaiah b. Delaiah tried to frighten him by saying that his life was threatened (Neh. 6.10-13). Apparently Shemaiah was a prophet (cf. v. 12). Nehemiah concludes that he was hired by Tobiah and Sanballat, but this could just have been an opinion; for all we know, Shemaiah was telling the truth, or perhaps he was trying to frighten Nehemiah because he personally opposed him without any prompting from anyone else. Similarly, Nehemiah pronounces a curse 'against Noadiah the prophetess and against the other prophets' who were trying to intimidate him (v. 14).

The opposition did not stop here but came from the very heart of the Jerusalem establishment (Neh. 6.17-19). Various of the nobles (חרים) communicated by letter with Tobiah. These men had access to Nehemiah and spoke well of Tobiah to him. This suggests that these individuals were hardly intractable enemies of Nehemiah, as one might think from the tenor of the text. They seem to have been on reasonable terms with him even if not agreeing with his attempts to cut ties with certain of the surrounding peoples. They appear to have been more tolerant of Nehemiah than he of them. In sum, the established Jewish leadership clearly took a rather different view from Nehemiah's.

Finally, the 'priest' Eliashib assigned a large room in the Temple area to Tobiah who was a relative (Neh. 13.4-13). The indication is that Eliashib was in fact the High Priest and had responsibility over the entire Temple (cf. Neh. 3.1, 20; 13.28). As governor, Nehemiah was able to have Tobiah turfed out and also to effect other changes having to do with the Temple organization. He justifies this by claiming that Levites were not carrying out their duties and the tithes were not being collected. Whether this was true cannot be known, of course, since we have only his side of the story. What he does indicate is that trade in Jerusalem was strictly regulated (Neh. 13.15-22). We can only assume that many Jews did not agree with his regulations, which were imposed by force.

The very end of the book of Nehemiah (13.4-31) is unlikely to be part of the Nehemiah Memoir,[13] but the matter is disputed. Whatever the case, two interesting claims are made (13.23-28). One is that Jews were marrying women from Ashdod, Ammon and Moab, and that Nehemiah forcibly broke up the families, even committing physical violence against some individuals. The other is that one of the sons of the High Priest married the daughter of Sanballat and was driven away by Nehemiah. Both of these suggest that his attempts to isolate the *golah* community from the native inhabitants could be maintained only when he was present and used the force available to him from his commission by the Persians. His reforms were evidently not a popular measure supported by the generality of the community.[14]

The 'Foreigners' and 'Peoples of the Lands'
Both Ezra and Nehemiah speak openly of 'foreigners' (Neh 9.1-2) and of the 'peoples of the land(s)' (Neh 10.1, 29-32) as those with whom the Jews have intermarried. According to one understanding of the Hebrew wording, these peoples were 'the Canaanites, the Hittites, the Perizzites, the Jebusites, the Ammonites, the Moabites, the Egyptians, and the Amorites' (Ezra 9.1-2).[15] Some of them were certainly identified with the Ammonites and the Moabites (Neh. 13.3).

There are reasons to doubt this picture. The Babylonians took Jerusalem twice in the early sixth century BCE, once in 597 and again in 587/586. On both these occasions, as well as possibly a third time, about 581, some of the population was taken captive to Mesopotamia (2 Kgs 24.14-16; Jer. 52.28-30). The number given by the text varies considerably between the sources, being a total of 10,000 or 8,000 according to 2 Kings but 4,600 according to Jeremiah. The reliability of these figures might be questioned, but the point to be taken here is

13. See P. Ackroyd, *The Age of the Chronicler* (Supplement to *Colloquium: The Australian and New Zealand Theological Review*; Auckland, New Zealand, 1970), pp. 28, 41.

14. Here I disagree with Kenneth D. Tollefson and H.G.M. Williamson, 'Nehemiah as Cultural Revitalization: an Anthropological Perspective', *JSOT* 56 (1992), pp. 41-68, especially p. 60, that the reform movement had 'attracted the backing of the bulk of the population' by the time of the mixed marriage issue.

15. Another understanding is that found, for example, in the New Jewish Publication Society translation: 'The people of Israel... have not separated themselves from the peoples of the land whose abhorrent practices are like those of the Canaanites, the Hittites...' Williamson, *Ezra, Nehemiah*, pp. 130-31, argues similarly.

that the portion of the population removed from the land was only a fraction of the total population. The bulk of the Jews remained in Palestine and were still there half a century later when some of the descendants of those taken captive were allowed to return by Persian decree (cf. Ezra 1.2-4).

Surprisingly, neither Ezra nor Nehemiah anywhere recognizes that the land was populated by Jews and that the returnees were only a minority. On the contrary, they give the impression that the *golah* came from Babylonia into a land which was more or less empty. Why? The answer seems to be that the only proper Jewish community was that formed of the returnees; the descendants of those who remained in the land were apparently considered illegitimate. Otherwise, the silence of Ezra and Nehemiah about them is inexplicable.

The 'Canaanites, the Hittites, the Perizzites, the Jebusites, the Ammonites, the Moabites, the Egyptians, and the Amorites' (Ezra 9.1-2) were traditional enemies of Israel (Exod. 3.8, 17; 23.23; 33.2; 34.11; Deut. 7.1; 20.17; Josh. 9.1; 17.15; 24.11; etc.), forming a stereotypical list. It is unlikely that identifiable ethnic groups still existed in Palestine at this time, even if they ever existed.[16] The most likely situation is that at least some of the 'peoples of the lands' were Jewish descendants of those not taken captive during the reign of Nebuchadnezzar. In other words, Ezra and Nehemiah regarded any marriage with these people as a breach of the law. If so, this was a very narrow and problematic interpretation of the law. No wonder there was so much opposition!

The place of Samaria in this picture is especially problematic.

---

16. A case can be made that the nations alleged to be in Canaan and driven out or conquered by Israel were largely a literary fiction. For example, the Rephaim were supposedly one of the ancient inhabitants of the land (e.g. Gen. 14.5; 15.20; Deut. 2.11, 20; 3.11, 13), yet in the Ugaritic texts they are the deceased ancestors (cf. *KTU* 1.21 = Aqhat IVa; *KTU* 1.161 = ritual text?). Also, Og of Bashan, labelled as a remnant of the Rephaim, dwells in Ashtarot and Edrei (Deut. 1.4; 3.10-11; Josh. 9.10; 12.4; 13.12), the same area in which the god Rapha'u of a Ugaritic incantation seems to dwell (*KTU* 1.108). It appears that myth has been historicized, and the shades have been turned into ethnographical entities. Other passages (such as Job 26.5; Ps. 88.11-13; Isa. 26.14, 19; Prov. 9.18) associate the Rephaim with the dead. This is only some of the evidence which suggests that the biblical picture of the Canaanites is very much a literary creation, produced to support the ideology of the text; see N.P. Lemche, *The Canaanites and their Land: The Tradition of the Canaanites* (JSOTSup, 110; Sheffield: Sheffield Academic Press, 1991).

Commentators have often interpreted Sanballat and those around him in the light of later Jewish anti-Samaritan polemic. It is very unclear, however, that the antipathy between the Jewish community and the Gerizim community had yet developed; on the contrary, such antagonism is attested no earlier than the Seleucid period and possibly much later (see the section on 'The Hasmonaeans' below). Likewise, the relationship between Sanballat and the Gerizim community is uncertain. All we can say is that Sanballat was a Yahwist and had close ties with some Jews, such as Tobiah. Whether he had anything to do with the community later associated with the cult on Gerizim is unknown.

In sum, the 'foreigners' and the 'peoples of the land(s)' were an undifferentiated mass placed by the compilers of Ezra and Nehemiah in opposition to the pure community—the 'holy seed' (Ezra 9.2)—made up of those who had returned from the purifying fire of the Exile. They were the people who lived in the land when 'the remnant' (Ezra 9.8, 15) came from Babylonia and settled there. The fact that many of those living in the land were Jews themselves, descendants of those left when Nebuchadnezzar exiled a certain portion of the population, is completely ignored by Ezra and Nehemiah.

The Ptolemaic Period[17]

In spite of the great gaps in our knowledge of Persian Judah, we do have the biblical books, which reveal attitudes and outlooks, if not always reliable data about events. For the Ptolemaic period we have hardly anything, apart from two sources of rather different value: the Zenon papyri which give us a peephole into Palestine about 259 BCE, and Josephus's version of the Tobiad romance (*Ant.*12.4.1-11 §§157-236). The Zenon papyri reveal to us a Tobias who was an influential local ruler and commander over a *katoikos* or settlement of soldiers in the Transjordanian area. The Tobiad romance tells of the adventures of his son Joseph and grandson Hyrcanus (or possibly they are Tobias's grandson and great grandson); the details should be accepted only with great caution, but the general outline of the story seems credible.

Neither of these sources says much about religious practices in

17. For a more detailed discussion of much of the information in this section, see chapter 4 of my *Judaism from Cyrus to Hadrian.* I. *Persian and Greek Periods*; II. *Roman Period* (Minneapolis: Fortress Press, 1992; one volume edn London: SCM, 1994).

Judah during this time. Yet they do describe a situation in which the Jewish leadership seems to be at home in the Ptolemaic world. Tobias sends gifts of slaves to Apollonius, the finance minister of Ptolemy II Philadelphus, and gifts of exotic animals to Ptolemy himself. His correspondence is in Greek and, even though he undoubtedly employed a Greek scribe, he is likely to have known some of the language. One of his letters gives 'many thanks to the gods' (*pollē charis tois theois*), a conventional phrase inserted by the secretary but unlikely to have been done without Tobias's knowledge.

The Tobiad romance confirms this picture. Both Joseph and later his son Hyrcanus communicate in Greek and conduct themselves in the cosmopolitan Ptolemaic court as to the manner born. They also seem to find no affront to their religious sensibilities, banqueting alongside the other local dignitaries in the king's presence. Joseph Tobiad had friends in Samaria from whom he was able to borrow money when the need arose (*Ant.* 12.4.3 §168). Whatever the believability of the account's details, the author of the story has certainly painted a picture of a family that exemplifies the very attitudes opposed by Ezra and Nehemiah.

Of course, one can object that the Tobiads were not typical of all Jews, and this is true.[18] They were a wealthy, upper-class family with the opportunities and means of a Greek education, not to mention the incentives to want to obtain such. Most Jews were not wealthy or upper class. But the assumption that the Tobiads had somehow compromised their religion does not necessarily follow. On the contrary, they had intermarried with the high-priestly family, the Oniads. Joseph was himself the nephew of the high priest Onias (probably Onias II). The relationship continued, for during the reign of Seleucus IV (187–175 BCE) Hyrcanus had a large sum of money on deposit in the Jerusalem Temple, with the authorization of the High Priest Onias III (2 Macc. 3.11), even though Judah was at that time under Seleucid rule, while Hyrcanus was a Ptolemaic supporter (see next section).

The 'sheiks' or local village rulers were an important feature of Ptolemaic Palestine,[19] and here Tobias does not seem untypical.

---

18. See L.H. Feldman, who speaks of the 'highly assimilated—and highly exceptional—family of the Tobiads' in 'Hengel's *Judaism and Hellenism* in Retrospect', *JBL* 96 (1977), pp. 371-82. See also my comments on Feldman's article in *Judaism from Cyrus to Hadrian*, I, p. 151.

19. V. Tcherikover, 'Palestine Under the Ptolemies (A Contribution to the Study

Another of the Zenon papyri tells of a local ruler named Jeddous (Hebrew, *Yeddua*) to whom Zenon sent an official to collect a debt. Jeddous sent them packing:

> [Alexan]dros to Oryas, greeting. I have received your letter, to which you added a copy of the letter written by Zenon to Jeddous saying that unless he gave the money to Straton, Zenon's man, we were to hand over his pledge to him (Straton). I happened to be unwell as a result of taking some medicine, so I sent a lad, a servant of mine, with Straton, and wrote a letter to Jeddous. When they returned they said that he had taken no notice of my letter, but had attacked them and thrown them out of the village. So I am writing to you (for your information).[20]

Only an extremely foolhardy man or one with a good deal of confidence in his own autonomy would have dared defy the agent (Zenon) of the Ptolemaic finance minister who was second only to the king himself. Alexander had little stomach for confronting Jeddous and developed a diplomatic illness. He seems to have anticipated Jeddous's rough reception of Zenon's man. We know little of ordinary Jews, but at least some of those in Tobias's military colony seem to have been Jews. They would have lived alongside non-Jews from a variety of backgrounds and origins. As has been demonstrated at length, the Ptolemaic administration reached down to the deepest level of society, even if it was through local administrators such as Jeddous and Tobias.[21]

Thus, what little information we have of this period does not show Judah or its inhabitants as any different from other peoples under Ptolemaic rule.

The Jerusalem 'Hellenistic Reform'[22]

When Antiochus III took Palestine for the Seleucids in 200 BCE, things continued much as they had been, according to all the information available to us. Antiochus issued a decree acknowledging help

of the Zenon Papyri)', *Mizraim* 4-5 (1937), pp. 9-90, especially pp. 49-51.

20. Translation in *CPJ* I.6 (p. 130).

21. The classic study is that of M. Hengel, *Judaism and Hellenism: Studies in their Encounter in Palestine during the Early Hellenistic Period* (2 vols.; London: SCM Press; Philadelphia: Fortress Press, 1974). The main issues and data are surveyed in Chapter 3 of my *Judaism from Cyrus to Hadrian*.

22. Detailed discussion on the points in this section can be found in Chapter 5 of my *Judaism from Cyrus to Hadrian*.

from the Jews in taking Jerusalem and affirming their right to continue to live by their usual customs (Josephus, *Ant.* 12.3.3-4 §§138-46).
These rights had been negotiated by John the father of Eupolemus (1
Macc. 8.17; 2 Macc. 4.11). The High Priest was Simon (II), apparently the son of the Onias known from the Tobiad romance (Sir. 50).
The priesthood, Temple, and cult continued without any change; the
only change was that of overlord.

Change came when Antiochus IV, the son of Antiochus III and
brother of Seleucid IV, took the throne in 175; however, he was not
the initiator of the change. Rather, the current High Priest (Onias III)
had a brother Joshua or Jason who desired the office for himself. He
offered to pay a large sum to Antiochus for the right to become High
Priest; furthermore, he paid an additional sum to turn Jerusalem into
a *polis* or city with a Greek constitution.

Much has been made of this reform, usually following the negative
tone of 1 and 2 Maccabees, which regard the events under Jason as the
height of impiety. But, of course, 1 and 2 Maccabees were written in
the aftermath of the suppression of worship by Antiochus seven years
later and the subsequent successful revolt of the Jewish people against
this oppression. Yet even their very biased stance with regard to Jason
cannot hide the fact that his 'Hellenistic reform' was widely supported
within Jerusalem—1 and 2 Maccabees can point to no opposition to
it.[23] On the contrary, all the evidence we have points to the active
acceptance of the Greek constitution by the inhabitants of Jerusalem,
many of whom became citizens.

As far as religious practice is concerned, we have no indication of
any changes. The Temple still functioned, the daily sacrifices were still
offered, Jason still evidently carried out his priestly duties. Despite its
emotive language, containing such words as 'unlawful' (*paranomous*),
'ungodly' (*asebous*), 'wickedness' (*anagneian*), and the like, 2 Maccabees 4 cannot point to any actual violation of Jewish law. Whatever
his transgression in usurping the high priesthood, Jason remained—
and viewed himself—as a faithful and loyal member of the Jewish
religion.[24] The governmental structure had changed, but religious

23. The oft-made statement that 'the pious Jews were outraged' is sheer speculation—there is not a shred of evidence for this statement. That there was a variety of
reactions among the Jews would not be surprising, but the sources are absolutely
silent.

24. The only possible violation of law in the account of 2 Maccabees (whose

observance continued as before. Nehemiah would have been horrified, but he would have been a minority.

Hasmonaeans

One might think that attitudes would have changed drastically once the nation had experienced the Seleucid religious suppression and the Maccabean revolt. The cleansing of the Temple and the restoration of the sacrificial cult was an occasion of great rejoicing. One might have supposed that the reaction would be to turn to a position like that in the books of Ezra and Nehemiah—for the people to cut outside ties and become inward looking. Some may have favoured this approach, judging from some of the Jewish literature of this time. The Qumran community can be interpreted as taking this route, though there is still much uncertainty about the community. There were also those who construed the shocking attack on their religion as a sign of the end of time (e.g. the writer of Daniel 7–12), so their focus was undoubtedly on their narrow community.

The Hasmonaeans were set on extending the boundaries of Judah, and either ousting the natives or converting them to Judaism by force. They thus followed a policy of ridding their realm of 'pagan' worship. This included the destruction of the Samaritan temple on Gerizim according to Josephus (*Ant.* 13.9.1 §§255-56). Yet the Hasmonaeans also actively sought ties with the surrounding nations. Already Judas allegedly attempted to make an agreement with Rome (1 Macc. 8.23-32), and Jonathan corresponded with the Spartans (1 Macc. 12.5-23). In none of their activities do they appear to make Judah into the isolationist regime so beloved of Nehemiah and his supporters.

author would have leapt on the smallest deviance with glee) is found in 4.18-20. According to the story here, Jason sent money to have pagan sacrifices offered at Tyre. However, according to the story itself, the money was not used for that purpose. The explanation given is that the messengers gave the money to purchase warships, despite Jason's intent. This is incredible: with such a large sum of money Jason would have chosen his messengers with care; for them to use the money contrary to his instructions seems extremely unlikely. The most logical explanation is that Jason sent the money specifically for warships, but the author of 2 Maccabees put the worst possible interpretation on the deed. For more information on the 'Hellenistic Reform', see my article, 'The Hellenistic City of Jerusalem' in Sean Freyne (ed.) *Jews in Hellenistic Cities* (London: Routledge, forthcoming).

A good example of this is Eupolemus. As noted above, his father John had negotiated the transfer of Judah from Ptolemaic to Seleucid rule, with the maintenance of her traditional customs and religion (1 Macc. 8.17; 2 Macc. 4.11). These passages state that Eupolemus was sent by Judas as an ambassador to negotiate a treaty with Rome. This suggests a man with a good education and the ability to handle himself in an international situation. It is widely believed that Eupolemus was the author of a history of the Jews which has come down to us only in fragments.[25] This was written in Greek and contained an interpretation of biblical history which draws on a variety of traditions, including not only the Hebrew Bible but also the Septuagint translation, and it has a Hellenistic colouring in some passages. Even Eupolemus's name was Greek. Although the Maccabees represented a robust nationalistic movement, the Hasmonaean rulers had a distinctly international outlook and set of policies. It has been noted correctly that the Hasmonaean court seems a typical Hellenistic court of the time.

The Samaritans are a complication to this picture. At some point, attempts were made by the Jewish community to exclude the adherents of the Gerizim cult from regular association. It is during the Seleucid and Hasmonaean periods that we may begin to find evidence of antagonism to a cultic community centred on the temple on Mount Gerizim; however, no compelling evidence for a major breach occurs earlier than the first century CE.[26] Even in the rabbinic period, the indication is that a kinship between Jews and Samaritans was recognized.[27] The Samaritan community always presented problems because it was not clearly pagan but also did not owe loyalty to Jerusalem or the Jewish religious authorities in whatever period is in question.

---

25. For the text, translation, and extensive notes and discussion, see C.R. Holladay, *Fragments from Hellenistic Jewish Authors. I. Historians* (Texts and Translations, 20; Pseudepigrapha Series, 10; Atlanta, Scholars Press, 1983), pp. 93-156.

26. See L.L. Grabbe, 'Betwixt and Between: The Samaritans in the Hasmonaean Period', in E.H. Lovering, Jr (ed.), *Society of Biblical Literature 1993 Seminar Papers* (SBLSP, 32; Atlanta: Scholars Press, 1993), pp. 334-47. See also R.J. Coggins, *The Samaritans and the Jews* (London: Basil Blackwell; Atlanta: John Knox Press, 1975), pp. 57-74, 162-64; Gunneweg, *Esra*, p. 79.

27. See L. Schiffman, 'The Samaritans in Tannaitic Halakhah', *JQR* 75 (1984–85), pp. 323-50.

Conclusions

It seems strangely ironic that scholars have held up the reforms of
Ezra–Nehemiah as examples of piety, yet in their own twentieth-
century context would pride themselves on their tolerance, their
broadmindedness, and their view that religions other than Christianity
and Judaism have integrity and should be respected. However, my aim
has not been to try to pass a verdict on the views found in Ezra and
Nehemiah. Whether the reforms of Ezra–Nehemiah were good or bad
is not a judgment that can be made by scholarship. It is essentially a
question for the theologian or, more particularly, the believer. The
question is irrelevant for the historian. So whether Nehemiah can be
seen as an model of piety or as a mere xenophobe depends on a very
subjective reaction. As historians, however, what we can say is that
the reforms described in Ezra and Nehemiah were in many ways an
aberration in the history of Second Temple Judaism.

Nehemiah seems to have been distrustful of the Jerusalem leadership
from the beginning, and even his own account admits that he was
opposed by many of those in Jerusalem, even up to the very High
Priest himself. Strangely, the marriages he broke up by threat of
force were most likely those to descendants of those Jews who had not
been taken captive in 587 BCE. The community of those who returned
from Babylon was seen by some as the only legitimate community, but
others evidently took a different view. Nehemiah's reforms were temporary, lasting only as long as he could maintain them by force. In the
following centuries, the glimpses we have of the Jewish community,
sporadic as they are, seem to suggest a community that took a rather
different view from that of Nehemiah.

It would naturally be erroneous to suggest that the attitude of Jews
during the Second Temple period could be summed up in a brief,
simplistic sentence. We have to reckon with a variety of attitudes;
indeed, a complex of attitudes might exist even within the same individual. But our evidence indicates that the Jews of Judaea as a whole
were faithful to their religion, were not particularly happy with being
under foreign rule,[28] but also found plenty to do without pursuing

28. This may occasionally have taken the form of reacting to the cultural symbols
of that rule, but this is rather different from rejecting wholesale the culture itself. See
Grabbe, *Judaism from Cyrus to Hadrian*, pp. 163-64.

ideological chimeras. As a whole they did not reject the surrounding Persian or Hellenistic culture or attempt to isolate themselves from the world around.

Of course, this does not mean that there did not exist individuals or groups who would have followed Nehemiah's example, but they seem to have been in a minority, at least until the 66–70 CE revolt. The Temple captain (*strategos*), Eleazer b. Ananias, who stopped the traditional sacrifices for the Emperor in 66 would have been a man after Nehemiah's own heart (Josephus, *War* 2.17.2 §409). Perhaps in that sense, Nehemiah won in the end, but at this point Judaea's time as a nation was about up. Beginning with the destruction of the Temple in 70 and culminating in the aftermath of the 132–35 revolt, the Jewish religious picture changed drastically. The new situation demanded new values and a new conceptionalization about Jewish identity, even if the tradition itself could be drawn on to provide convenient antecedents.[29]

29. Since this article went to press, an important monograph on the question of the 'people of the land' in Ezra–Nehemiah has appeared: Hans M. Barstad, *The Myth of the Empty Land: A Study in the History and Archaeology of Judah During the 'Exilic' Period* (Symbolae Osloenses, 28; Oslo: Scandinavian University Press, 1996). Also a more lengthy discussion of many points made about Ezra and Nehemiah can be found in my *Ezra–Nehemiah* (Readings; London: Routledge, 1998 forthcoming).

JEWISH LOCAL PATRIOTISM: THE SAMARITAN PROBLEM*

Richard Coggins

There is something of an irony in the fact that an essay on the theme of Samaritan patriotism is being completed at the time (February 1996) of what must surely be the first ever venture by the Samaritan community into participatory democracy. Some three hundred voters, and three candidates, have been taking part in the elections to the inaugural Palestinian legislative council on the Palestinian West Bank, and the electoral system has been structured so as to ensure that the Samaritan candidate with the most votes will be assured of a seat, even though the electorate is tiny by comparison with that for most seats. The distinctiveness of the Samaritans, as neither Arab nor Israeli, is thereby acknowledged. But it is also worthy of note that all three candidates were from the priestly families which continue to play a major part in the community's affairs. Thus it becomes clear that the age-long issue of whether the Samaritans are more properly to be understood as an ethnic or a religious group remains a moot point.

Such it has been since at least the turn of the eras, and it confronts us with an immediate difficulty when we try to reach an understanding of the Samaritan standpoint in the issue of local patriotism. Just as there is a contemporary ambiguity, so when Samaritan history is studied there is no agreement as to whether they are more properly understood as a group whose primary bonds were those of ethnicity or those of a religious community. In addition, the confusion and uncertainty which continue to bedevil our understanding of the last centuries BCE and the first of our era provide their own particular problems. There is still no general agreement as to the point at which

*   I attended the Conference at which many of the papers in this volume were presented, but was then very much an observer, being newly retired. I am grateful to Dr Sarah Pearce for her invitation to contribute to the published papers of the Conference.

it becomes legitimate to speak of a distinctive Samaritan community.

There is a further ambiguity, inherent in any discussion of local patriotism, which must certainly be borne in mind. It can be illustrated by what may seem a rather far-fetched parallel. Since 1940 the word 'quisling' has often been used to denote someone regarded as unpatriotic, a betrayer of the true interests of one's country. The word derives from the name of a Norwegian politician, Vidkun Quisling, who cooperated with the Nazis when they invaded his country in that year. He came to be regarded as a traitor, motivated only by the hope of personal advancement under the hegemony of Nazi Germany. But it would obviously be possible to argue that he was motivated by feelings of patriotism, a conviction that the best future for his country lay in close cooperation with the Third Reich.

The parallel is certainly distant and may seem totally irrelevant, but it is chosen deliberately. During the period with which we are concerned in our study of Samaritan patriotism, Palestine came under the control of two different foreign powers: the Seleucid Empire of Antioch, and the Romans. The literary evidence relating to the impact of these powers comes from Judah; there are no likely Samaritan literary survivals.

Two important points relevant to our immediate concern need to be taken into account with regard to this Jewish evidence. First, if any allusion or direct reference to the Samaritans is made, it is likely to be an unsympathetic one. Scholars have rightly become more cautious than was formerly the case in speaking of a 'Samaritan schism', as if that were an event which happened at some specific date. What we can say is that over an extended period relations between Jerusalem Jewry and the Samaritans became at best tense, and were often downright hostile. When we also bear in mind that the literature in question is for the most part of a religious nature and we recall that religion characteristically brings out the most bitter animosities in humanity, we shall see with what care such evidence needs to be treated. Fortunately anti-Samaritan polemic was less embittered during the period with which we are concerned than it later became.

Secondly, with regard to the Seleucids in particular, we must also remember that the Jewish evidence which has come down to us presents one unambiguous viewpoint: to cooperate with the Seleucids was wrong, a betrayal of the community's heritage, a lack of patriotism. Daniel 11–12 spells out the course of events, but only in oblique terms, for it is written as if they were still in the future. 1 and 2 Maccabees labour under no such handicap, and despite their internal differences, they are agreed on the folly of Antiochus IV's ambitions, and the wickedness of those members of the community who did anything that might further those ambitions. The kind of Hellenism promoted by Antiochus was utterly alien to Judaism and all its traditions. Those who supported Antiochus were craven betrayers of true Judaism. Patriotism meant resistance to the Seleucid forces.

That, at least, is the virtually unanimous verdict of the literary survivals. But is this the whole story? Is it indeed anything more than the presentation of one ideology? Many modern scholars have focused on those elements in our sources which suggest that the picture was a much more complex one than that suggested by 1 Maccabees in particular, and they maintain that it is possible to detect a whole range of attitudes toward Hellenism in the Judaism of the period.[1]

It is not appropriate in this context to go into that issue in greater detail, but even so brief a sketch should serve as a reminder that when we are considering patriotism we must be aware of the two levels of concern. Patriotism may, of course, be understood at the level of loyal membership of one's own local communtiy, be it Jerusalem Jewish or Samaritan, and there may be circumstances in which the verdict of history comes to be that only at that level can there be true loyalty. To cooperate with 'outsiders' is to risk utter condemnation in the history of one's own community. Vidkun Quisling in our own century has received as decisively negative a verdict as did the 'sinful people, men who were renegades', who cooperated with Antiochus IV's plans in 1 Macc. 1.34.

But from a different point of view it is easy to envisage that true patriotism might imply being a loyal subject of the larger empire. Thus, in the period of the Roman Empire, it was not implausible to claim that true patriotism meant loyalty to that Empire, not least as being one way of ensuring freedom of religious practice. The evidence of the New Testament provides an interesting parallel here:

---

1. See in particular M. Hengel, *Judaism and Hellenism: Studies in their Encounter in Palestine during the Early Hellenistic Period* (2 vols.; London: SCM Press; Philadelphia: Fortress Press, 1974), and L.L. Grabbe, *Judaism from Cyrus to Hadrian*. I. *Persian and Greek Periods* and II. *Roman Period* (Minneapolis: Fortress Press, 1992; London: SCM Press, 1994 [one-volume edn]), of which Chapter 3 is devoted to a full discussion of this topic.

such passages as Rom. 13.1-7 and 1 Pet. 2.13-14 indicate that there certainly was one strand within early Christianity which preached (and presumably practised) loyal cooperation with the imperial authorities. This is not unconnected with the fact that the Roman Empire proved to be a story of lasting success in a way that the Seleucids were not. Those who supported the Seleucids were to receive a negative verdict from history; to be a loyal member of the Roman Empire was a different story. It is perhaps at this point that we recall that probably the best known quotations embodying the word 'patriotism' are Edith Cavell's 'Patriotism is not enough' and Dr Johnson's description of patriotism as 'the last refuge of a scoundrel'. Patriotism has its limitations; it can also hide a variety of less obviously attractive motivations.

The Samaritan Situation

It is time to turn more specifically to the Samaritan situation. I will first look briefly at Samaritan patriotism as expressed in attitudes to the ruling power. The brevity is required by that lack of clear evidence to which I have already alluded. Then it will be appropriate to give slightly fuller attention to the question of patriotism expressed in terms of Samaritan self-awareness—the awareness of belonging to a specific group whose true 'home' was Mount Gerizim, the holy mountain close to Shechem, which the existing community still venerates.

The most obviously relevant text relating to Samaritan attitudes to Hellenization is 2 Macc. 6.2, which sets out in parallel the requirements of the Seleucid authorities with regard to the two temples, in Jerusalem and on Mount Gerizim.[2] What seems like a characteristic piece of anti-Samaritan polemic suggests that those who live around Mount Gerizim already describe their temple as dedicated to Zeus-the-Friend-of-Strangers, as if they can be dismissed as unpatriotic through their readiness to accept Hellenistic practices. But such a reading of the text raises problems on at least two grounds. First, it involves the issue I have already noted, of accepting as straightforward historical description an assertion which must surely be understood as ideologi-

---

2. The textual difficulties as to the identity of the royal emissary (LXX, *geronta Athenaion*; NRSV, 'an Athenian senator', with the marginal notes that 'Antiochian' is a possible alternative reading for 'Athenian', and that 'Geron' might be understood as a proper name) need not here detain us.

cal, a piece of polemic aimed against the Samaritans. Secondly, it ignores the larger context of 2 Maccabees itself, which has made clear a few verses earlier (5.22-23) that the Gerizim community was as much the subject of oppression by the Imperial authorities as were the Jerusalem Jews. In the larger context it is the Seleucid authorities rather than the Samaritans who are being condemned; anti-Samaritan expression surfaces only in the final notes, 'as did the people who lived in that place'.[3]

A well-known additional complication relating to these events is provided by Josephus, whose hostility to the Samaritans is well established. At *Ant.* 12.5.5 §§257-64 he quotes a letter allegedly sent to Antiochus by 'the Sidonians in Shechem', maintaining that though they share many religious practices with the Jews they are in fact of entirely different origin ('we are Sidonians by origin'), distinct from the Jews both in race and in customs. They request that their temple on Mount Gerizim be known as that of 'Zeus Hellenios' and that the persecution against them should be suspended. Josephus goes on to quote a reply from Antiochus acceding to these requests.[4]

Grabbe, in his discussion of these texts, accepts that the letters are probably genuine, but, following on his doubts concerning the interpretation of 2 Macc. 6.2 (see n. 3 below), he questions the rightness of the obvious immediate conclusion: that the Samaritans themselves were willing, or even eager, for their cult to be Hellenized. He maintains that they certainly wished to distance themselves from the Jerusalem Jews and did this by suggesting a separate origin; in other respects, however, they were anxious to retain the distinctive features of the cult, such as Sabbath observance and worship at their temple, to both of which their letter refers. Grabbe may indeed be right, though it is possible that here he gives insufficient weight to the often

3.   A possible alternative understanding of this verse is favoured by L.L. Grabbe, 'Betwixt and Between: The Samaritans in the Hasmonean Period', in E.H. Lovering, Jr (ed.), *Society of Biblical Literature 1993 Seminar Papers* (SBLSP, 32; Atlanta: Scholars Press, 1993), pp. 334-47. He supposes that the reference may well be to the hospitable practice of the community at Gerizim rather than a renaming of their temple. In the larger context of anti-Samaritan polemic this does not seem wholly persuasive. (I am grateful to Professor Grabbe for letting me have a copy of this paper, which is to be published in the next series of Second Temple Studies in the JSOT Supplement Series, see previous chapter n. 26.)

4.   Text and translation in R. Marcus (ed.), *Josephus*, VII (LCL; Cambridge, MA: Harvard University Press; London: Heinemann, 1961), §§133-37.

expressed anti-Samaritanism of Josephus. For Josephus, the alleged Samaritan tendency to link themselves with the Jews in times of prosperity and to deny any such linkage in times of adversity is part of his sustained polemic against the community. It says little about the reality or otherwise of Samaritan 'patriotism' vis-à-vis the ruling power of the day.

When we turn to Samaritan attitudes toward the Roman authorities at a slightly later date, Josephus in practice offers our only literary evidence, and it must be subject to cautions relating not only to Josephus's hostility toward the Samaritans (which is actually less prominent in his discussion of the Roman period in *Antiquities*), but also to his apologetic intention in justifying Judaism to his Roman readers.

There are two main events described in *Antiquities* that illustrate Samaritan attitudes to the ruling authorities in the first century of our era, together with some briefer references in the *Jewish War*.[5] In *Ant.* 18. 4.2-3 §§88-95, Josephus describes a disturbance relating to a claim that the 'hidden' Temple vessels were to be revealed on Mount Gerizim. The Roman ruler, Pontius Pilate, suspected a potential revolt against his authority and acted brutally against those whom he regarded as involved in rebellion. But any attempt on our part to see in this an example of Samaritan local patriotism asserting itself against the Roman oppressor is checked when we discover that the Samaritan authorities thereupon appealed to Pilate's superior, Vitellius the governor of Syria, and that this episode played a significant part in Pilate's recall to Rome. This is one of those passages in Josephus where there is no obvious anti-Samaritan feeling in his account; in recounting these events he seems more concerned to show the impartiality of Roman justice, which would not recoil from punishing its own officials if that were the proper course of action.

A second episode, mentioned in both *Ant.* 20.6.1-3 §§118-36 and *War* 2.12.3-7 §§232-46,[6] must have taken place some fifteen years later, in the early 50s CE. A quarrel between the Samaritans and Jewish pilgrims passing through Samaritan territory on their way to Jerusalem led to bloodshed. The Roman governor Cumanus intervened,

---

5. I have discussed the relevant passages in R. Coggins, 'The Samaritans in Josephus', in L. Feldman and G. Hata (eds.), *Josephus, Judaism and Christianity* (Detroit: Wayne State University Press, 1987), pp. 257-73.

6. Though there are divergences of detail it seems highly probable that both accounts refer to the same set of events.

largely vindicating the Samaritans. If Josephus's account is accepted, then it would seem a further clear pointer to the fact that Samaritan patriotism did not preclude recourse to the imperial authorities in the search for justice. In itself this would be a pointer toward understanding the Samaritans largely in religious rather than political terms, a point to which I must return later.

It is noteworthy that in the first of the two accounts mentioned above, that which took place at the time of Pontius Pilate, Josephus refers to the Samaritan *ethnos*. It might seem obvious, if we were to be literal in our translation, that there is here an ethnic rather than a purely religious issue. But whereas the Loeb translation renders *ethnos* as 'nation', that may give a slightly misleading impression; a more general rendering such as 'people' would probably convey the sense more appropriately.

With Josephus's brief references in the *Jewish War* to the Samaritan involvement in the war itself we need not here concern ourselves. In the crisis situation of the years following 66 CE, it would be very difficult to discern any underlying principles, patriotic or otherwise, at work. The main focus of the war came quickly to be Jerusalem; it is impossible to tell from the brief accounts in Josephus whether the Samaritans in any sense felt themselves to be in an 'anti-Roman' struggle. Nor indeed can we be certain how much Josephus actually knew of contemporary Samaritanism; his well-rehearsed religious 'pilgrimage', exploring different religious groups, will scarcely have taken him to Mount Gerizim![7]

The overall impression conveyed by the admittedly meagre sources of information concerning Samaritan attitudes to the ruling powers, Seleucid and Roman, is of a willingness to co-operate with those powers provided that their religious commitments could be maintained. There is little sense that the retention of their identity made any demand that they should resist imperial demands, or take an active part in such resistance when it was orchestrated by others. To that extent the impression of the Samaritans as a religious rather than an ethnic group is sustained.

---

7. This point is discussed by Feldman's introduction in Feldman and Hata (eds.), *Josephus, Judaism and Christianity*, pp. 23-67 (47-48).

Samaritan Self-awareness

I now turn to the other related issue with which this essay is concerned; that of Samaritan self-awareness. To some extent that issue must be bound up with the question of origins. Judaism in the larger sense has always made much of its awareness of its origins and its loyalty to them, and there is no reason to suppose that the Samaritans will have been any different in this respect.

The older, largely polemical, viewpoint, based on a surface reading of 2 Kings 17, that the Samaritans were of alien origin, whose roots could be traced back to the settlers introduced by the Assyrians in the eighth and succeeding centuries BCE, has largely been abandoned (though traces of it may still be found in unexpected places);[8] but it is still widely held that they represented the survival of the tradition of the one-time Northern Kingdom. As long ago as 1977, Pummer drew attention to the need for 'research into the question of possible links between ancient Northern Israelite religion and Samaritan religion',[9] and this can properly be seen as part of the larger question of the extent to which the Samaritans were the heirs of the one-time Northern Kingdom. In fact it now seems clear that the Samaritans were only one of a number of divergent groups to be found in that area. Egger has drawn attention to the varied usage in Josephus, both in her full-scale dissertation and in her briefer article devoted to the same topic.[10] She has attempted to show that references in Josephus to the

8. An assessment of 'la valeur historique de 2R 17,24-33' forms the concluding section of the article by M. Delcor, 'La divinité Ashima de Samarie en 2R 17,30 et ses survivances: Du paganisme au judaïsme samaritain', in A. Tal and M. Florentin (eds.), *Proceedings of the First International Congress of the Société d'Etudes Samaritaines, Tel-Aviv, Jerusalem, 1991* (Tel-Aviv: Chaim Rosenberg School for Jewish Studies/Tel-Aviv University, 1991), pp. 33-48.

9. R. Pummer, 'The Present State of Samaritan Studies II', *JSS* 22 (1977), pp. 27-47 (47). Grabbe, 'Betwixt and Between: The Samaritans', p. 344, says, 'I am not aware of significant arguments against the idea that the [Samaritan] cult was ultimately descended from the Yahwistic worship of the Northern Kingdom'. This lack of significant arguments is indeed true enough; the problem arises from the equal lack of significant arguments in the contrary sense.

10. R. Egger, *Josephus Flavius und die Samaritaner: Eine terminologische Untersuchung zur Identitätsklärung der Samaritaner* (NTOA, 4; Freiburg: Universitätsverlag, 1986); and 'Flavius Josephus and the Samaritans: Aspects of the Samaritans and of their Early History', in Tal and Florentin (eds.), *Proceedings*, pp. 109-14.

'Samareis' and to the 'Sidonians at Shechem' have nothing to do with those who came to be known as Samaritans, though whether Josephus was as consistent in his usage as she maintains must be open to question. In addition, her further point, that the Samaritan community can be traced as early as the fourth century BCE, would be challenged by many, but it is not of direct relevance to the present study. In any case, it is clear that Josephus was hostile to the Samaritans; varied sources underlying his work may be traced, but in its final form they have been brought together in a way that brings out his distrust of the community in his own time.

But alongside this basically ethnic understanding there is an alternative presentation, which sees the distinctiveness of the Samaritans in their particular mix of religious beliefs. That such beliefs contained a geographical, if not an ethnic, element is obviously implied in their veneration for the sacred shrine on Mount Gerizim: one very striking way of expressing local patriotism. Nevertheless, if when referring to 'patriotism' we imply membership of a distinct and identifiable national community, the Samaritan case becomes more ambiguous.

This particular ambiguity was recognized and explored by Dexinger in a contribution to a volume devoted to the issue of self-definition: 'Limits of Tolerance in Judaism: The Samaritan Example'.[11] In that essay he first of all provides a valuable discussion and survey of the question of Samaritan origins, with appropriate warnings against the use and misuse of 2 Kings 17. It is, however, the closing section that is of the most immediate relevance to the present topic. He outlines four religious and four political factors which were relevant to the issue of Jewish tolerance of Samaritanism, and which may help us in the attempt to discern the nature of Samaritan 'patriotism'.

The religious factors he mentions are the changed self-awareness of the returning (Jewish) exiles; the issue of mixed marriages, which was linked with ethnic concerns; cult centralization; and the legitimacy of rival claims to the priesthood. In the political sphere he notes political and economic rivalry between Samaria and Jerusalem; the existence of the temple on Mount Gerizim, with the blend of political and religious interests which that enterprise involved; and the destruction of that

11. In E.P. Sanders, A.I. Baumgarten and A. Mendelson (eds.), *Jewish and Christian Self-Definition*. II. *Aspects of Judaism in the Graeco-Roman Period* (London: SCM Press, 1981), pp. 88-114.

temple (by John Hyrcanus), which again brought in political and religious concerns.[12]

Dexinger's listing is valuable in many ways, but could be misleading if it were followed too slavishly. He speaks of 'the religious plane' and 'the political sphere', listing points in each category, but in fact, as his own expression makes clear, such a categorization can be artificial. He himself, by his reference to 'political and religious interests', shows clearly how closely intertwined the religious and political issues were. The place of the sanctuary on Mount Gerizim illustrates this most vividly. How are we to discriminate between religious and political reasons for the veneration in which this was held among Samaritans? As well attempt to disentangle the two when reflecting on Jewish veneration for the temple on Mount Zion. In each case an important symbolic function can readily be discerned, which can fairly be said to transcend the barriers which modern Western scholarship might wish to set up between religious and political inspiration.

There is indeed a larger issue which must be alluded to, though it can hardly be explored in detail in this context. The use of the term 'Israel' within the Hebrew Bible itself is a notorious source of problems, and Van Seters has argued that the notion of 'all Israel' emerged following the overthrow of the Northern Kingdom of Israel by the Assyrians in 722: 'When Israel as a *political* state came to an end, Israel as a *religious* community came into being'.[13] This clearly raises complex questions concerning the whole intermix of political and religious identity during the Second Temple period that go far beyond the bounds of this essay.

In our immediate context, reference may properly be made at this point to the admittedly very scattered evidence from the Samaritan Diaspora. In 1979 two inscriptions were discovered on the Greek island of Delos that surely betray Samaritan origin. They are written in Greek, and the site on which they were found—close to that of the already known Jewish synagogue—was probably itself a synagogue.[14]

12. Dexinger, 'Limits of Tolerance', p. 113.

13. J. Van Seters, *In Search of History: Historiography in the Ancient World and the Origins of Biblical History* (New Haven: Yale University Press, 1983), p. 275.

14. A.T. Kraabel, 'New Evidence of the Samaritan Diaspora Has Been Found on Delos', *BA* 47 (1984), pp. 44-46. They are discussed twice by R. Pummer in A.D. Crown (ed.), *The Samaritans* (Tübingen: J.C.B. Mohr [Paul Siebeck], 1989), once under 'Samaritan Material Remains and Archaeology' (p. 150), and once under

Those who were responsible for the inscriptions describe themselves as *aparchomenoi eis hieron hagion Argarizein* (those who make offerings for the holy place Mount Gerizim). The date of the inscriptions is uncertain, but that is not of major importance for our present concern; the important point is that these settlers on Delos regarded themselves as bound to their homeland and specifically to the holy place, Mount Gerizim. We may note also that, as is usual with discoveries of this kind, it is impossible to say whether this was an isolated phenomenon, or whether it should be seen as a pointer to a widespread Samaritan Diaspora.

Striking though this evidence is, therefore, it does not resolve the duality I have been outlining. It would not be difficult on the one hand to regard the inscriptions as evidence of local patriotism in the sense of a community of traders and the like looking to its roots in a way familiar among diaspora communities of every kind down the ages. Alternatively, the specific reference to *argarizin* and the possibility that the building where the inscriptions were found was a synagogue might suggest a more specifically religious concern. We are indeed brought face to face with another long-standing problem: the extent to which it is legitimate to differentiate between religious and ethnic issues of this kind in the ancient world.

There is one other point with regard to the Delos discoveries which should be noted. Very close (less than 100 metres distant) to the site at which the *stelae* were found was a building which has been generally identified as a Jewish synagogue.[15] Only tentative conclusions can be based on such limited evidence, but it would be noteworthy, first, that two separate communities were involved. Samaritans and Jews each had their own focal point for meeting and worship. But then, secondly, it has been suggested that 'the proximity of the two structures does not suggest animosity between the two groups'.[16] This point may go somewhat beyond the evidence—proximity does not always

'Inscriptions' (pp. 193-94). Despite Pummer's own later warnings ('Argarizin: a Criterion for Samaritan Provenance?', *JSJ* 18 [1987], pp. 18-25), there seems to be no serious doubt that the Delos inscriptions do denote the existence of a Samaritan Diaspora in the Mediterranean world before the turn of the eras.

15. The possibility is not to be excluded that this building was itself a Samaritan synagogue, but those involved with working on the site regard this as the less probable identification (see Pummer, 'Samaritan Material Remains', p. 151).

16. R. W(hite), 'Delos', in A.D. Crown, R. Pummer and A. Tal (eds.), *A Companion to Samaritan Studies* (Tübingen: J.C.B. Mohr [Paul Siebeck], 1993), p. 69.

bespeak harmonious relations—but it is certainly to be noted. It is to be hoped that more evidence of the Samaritan Diaspora may come to light, since it is in the attitude of communities separated from their home-base that the role of patriotism can most readily be discerned, but at the moment that can be no more than a hope for the future.

Final Remarks

In recent years study of the New Testament has been radically reshaped by the contribution of different forms of social analysis. The whole idea of 'community' has come under scrutiny: the kind of social background from which early Christian groups emerged; their attitude to other apparently comparable religious groups; their setting within the larger structures of their time. It has been argued, for example, that vilification of enemies is one very important way of establishing self-identity as a community. This point, though made with reference to early Christianity, would certainly be relevant to Jewish attitudes toward Samaritans and, no doubt, if only there were any literary survivals, of Samaritan attitudes to Jews also.[17] Developments of a similar kind are beginning to take place in the study of Judaism (or, as Neusner never tires of pointing out, the 'many Judaisms') of the beginning of our era. In such a changing agenda the question of patriotism is a very natural one for consideration.

It may never be possible to reach a finally convincing view of Samaritan local patriotism until such sociological analysis has been carried out. Grabbe asserts, surely rightly, that 'To get at the sociology of the [Samaritan] community is not a simple matter'.[18] Indeed, it must remain doubtful, at best, whether such an analysis will ever be a realistic possibility in view of the paucity and the fragmentary nature of the available evidence, particularly the lack of Samaritan literary survivals which can plausibly be traced back to this period.[19] This

17. A useful survey of recent developments in this field, with bibliography, is provided by S. Barton, 'Community', in R.J. Coggins and J.L. Houlden (eds.), *A Dictionary of Biblical Interpretation* (London: SCM Press, 1990), pp. 134-38.

18. Grabbe, 'Betwixt and Between: The Samaritans', p. 334.

19. I have excluded from consideration here the fragments sometimes described as Pseudo-Eupolemos, or an 'Anonymous Samaritan'. The evidence that the author of this material was indeed a Samaritan is by no means convincing, and the fragments refer to the patriarchal material, from which it would in any case be very difficult to draw any confident conclusions with regard to our period. The relevant

uncertainty is the most basic reason for referring in the title of this paper to the Samaritan 'Problem'. Something can be achieved from the scrutiny of the way in which others, usually hostile, referred to the Samaritans, but in the absence of direct literary evidence from the Samaritans themselves the gaps in our understanding will inevitably remain considerable.

texts are to be found in J.H. Charlesworth (ed.), *The Old Testament Pseude-pigrapha* (London: Darton, Longman and Todd, 1985), II, pp. 873-82.

BELONGING AND NOT BELONGING:
LOCAL PERSPECTIVES IN PHILO OF ALEXANDRIA*

Sarah Pearce

Philo of Alexandria is one of the few Diaspora Jews about whose life-situation and personal views we know anything substantial. We are particularly fortunate, furthermore, in that this knowledge is transmitted in his own writings. He should, therefore, be treated as a central figure in any discussion about Diaspora Jewish attitudes towards the local environment. His elite social background and unprecedented intellectual achievement within ancient Judaism mean that his attitudes towards the local environment should not be read as representative of the perspective of Alexandrian Jews generally, though it is unwise to imagine that such a thing as a representative view may be constructed in any case. While Philo's attitude towards what he often called the 'Holy Land', with its focus in the Temple city, has received a certain amount of attention in modern scholarship,[1] the question of his attitudes to his homeland in Egypt has been less discussed, and has been considered mainly in the context of his rôle in the crisis for Alexandrian Jews in 38–41 CE. This leaves much room for further exploration.

This chapter looks at just two aspects relating to Philo's conception of his local environment. The first of these considers Philo's representation of Jewish identity over against Egyptian identity, and explores his generally very negative attitude towards Egypt and Egyptians.

*   I would like to thank Siân Jones and Tony Kushner for their helpful comments on this chapter. I am also most greatful to Martin Goodman and the Religions in the Mediterranean World Seminar at Wolfson College, Oxford, for what I learned from their generous response to a version of this paper.

1.   See especially B. Schaller, 'Philon von Alexandreia und das "Heilige Land"', in G. Strecker (ed.), *Das Land Israel in biblischer Zeit* (Göttingen: Vandenhoeck & Ruprecht, 1983), pp. 172-87.

This deals with an aspect of Philo's representation of Jewishness which, it seems to me, has often been overlooked in scholarship.[2] Recent work on cultural identity has shown that an opposition between 'us' and 'them' is an important dimension in the construction of group identity;[3] in the light of this approach, I look at how Philo represented Jewish identity in opposition to Egyptian identity as, at least in part, a political strategy in the historical circumstances of early Roman Egypt. The second section of this chapter explores to what extent Philo reveals a sense of attachment to his home city, Alexandria. Before looking at these two themes, however, it is necessary to locate Philo within the context of first-century Egypt, and to examine briefly the likely influences dominating his perspective on matters local.

Philo's Egypt

Philo's Egypt was a land which had undergone radical governmental and social change around the time of his birth (c. 20 BCE). In 30 BCE Octavian 'added Egypt to the empire of the Roman people',[4] reducing the once mighty Ptolemaic kingdom to what Philo described as the state of slavery.[5] Rome replaced Ptolemaic rule in Egypt with a Roman administration: this was supported by an army of occupation, and headed by a Roman prefect appointed both to secure the province as the source of grain for the city of Rome, and to prevent it being used again as a centre for Roman opposition to Octavian, as in the case of Antony's alliance with Cleopatra. In contrast to normal Roman policy which encouraged local self-government, the former royal capital of Alexandria was denied a city council, apparently on account of its citizens' hostility to Octavian. Citizens of Alexandria would reflect on their loss of political independence, and the reduction in status of Alexandria to a provincial city.

Of greatest consequence for the vast majority of Jews in Egypt,

---

2.   A notable exception is the useful, but brief, discussion of Jewish ideas about native Egyptians in the Hellenistic-Roman period by D. Zeller, 'Das Verhältnis der alexandrinischen Juden zu Ägypten', in M. Pye (ed.), *Religion in fremder Kultur: Religion als Minderheit in Europa und Asien* (Saarbrücken-Scheidt: Dadder, 1987), pp. 77-85.

3.   T.H. Eriksen, *Ethnicity and Nationalism: Anthropological Perspectives* (London: Pluto Press, 1993), pp. 18-35, 66.

4.   *Res Gestae* 27.

5.   Αἴγυπτός...νῦν ἐστι δούλη (*Jos.* 135).

however, was Octavian's repressive reorganization of Egyptian society, following a 'divide and rule' policy intended to 'keep the population strata as discrete and immutable as possible', and which greatly impeded upward social mobility.[6] This effectively dissolved the community of the 'Hellenes' which existed in Egypt under the Ptolemies, and in which the Jews and most people of immigrant, as opposed to native Egyptian, descent, had participated.[7] In its place Rome imposed a structure which sought to distinguish, and to keep separate, three social categories. At the top of the Roman social structure of Egypt were the holders of Roman citizenship. Beneath these were the citizens of the Greek cities of Egypt, including Alexandria, with social and financial privileges including exemption from the Roman poll-tax and straightforward access to Roman citizenship through their eligibility to serve in the Roman legions. Finally, below the two privileged social strata was the rest of the population, forming a 'vast third estate' to which most Jews and native Egyptians belonged.[8] Roman reorganization, while it favoured a small elite among the inhabitants of Egypt, effectively treated all without citizenship as Egyptians. How this reorganization affected the self-perception of these 'newly created "Egyptians"'[9] is an important question in connection with Philo's discussion of Jews and Egyptians.

Greek citizenship in Alexandria became a controversial issue as some sought to prove their eligibility for the citizen body;[10] disputes over the Greek citizenship of some Jews seem to have been an important

6.   N. Lewis, *Life in Egypt under Roman Rule* (Oxford: Clarendon Press, 1983), p. 32; on the social reorganization of Egypt, see Lewis, *Life in Egypt*, pp. 31-35; A. Bowman, 'Egypt', *Cambridge Ancient History* (Cambridge: Cambridge University Press, 2nd edn, 1996), X, Chapter 14b.

7.   On the destruction of the community of the Hellenes, see J. Mélèze Modrzejewski, 'Entre la cité et le fisc: Le statut grec dans l'Egypte romaine', in J. Mélèze Modrzejewski, *Droit impérial et traditions locales dans l'Egypte romaine* (Aldershot: Variorum Press, 1990), pp. 241-80 (252).

8.   Mélèze Modrzejewski, 'Entre la cité', p. 259.

9.   See the brief discussion on the Roman creation of 'ethnicity' in Roman Egypt by R.S. Bagnall, 'The Fayum and its People', in S. Walker and M. Bierbrier (eds.), *Ancient Faces: Mummy Portraits from Roman Egypt* (London: British Museum Press, 1997), pp. 17-20 (19).

10.   For the attempt of one Helenos, a Jew of Alexandria, who claimed Alexandria as his homeland (*patris*), to prove his eligibility as a citizen in the time of Augustus see *CPJ* II.151.

factor in communal tensions, which erupted into violent conflict in 38 CE.[11] For the vast majority of Alexandrian Jews who did not possess Greek citizenship, the new régime meant a severe reduction of status and the loss of a sense of belonging under Roman rule.[12] While Octavian permitted the Jews of Alexandria to maintain a degree of self-government in religious matters, such privileges will have been 'meagre concessions' and in no way comparable in status to that of the Greek citizen body.[13] Nevertheless, Rome's refusal to grant the citizens of Alexandria their own civic institutions may partly explain the increased hostility of some Alexandrian citizens against the Jews, if they regarded such privileges as the Jews had been granted with resentment,[14] though it is clear that the primary focus of widespread discontent in Alexandria and throughout Egypt was Rome.[15]

Philo's situation as an inhabitant of Alexandria must be seen in terms of his unusual elite social connections. He belonged to one of the few Jewish families whose members included citizens of Alexandria. As a historical actor, he became known for his rôle in the leadership of an embassy to Rome to protest over the unjust treatment of the Alexandrian Jews under the prefect Flaccus, and it is likely that a central part of his concerns was the treatment of those few Jews who

11.   This is suggested particularly by the evidence relating to the Alexandrian embassies, including that led by Philo, which took the dispute before the Roman emperor, see *CPJ* II.153, ll. 89-90; Josephus, *Ant.* 19.280-85; Josephus, *Apion* 2.38-72 (65).

12.   See V. Tcherikover, *Hellenistic Civilization and the Jews* (Philadelphia: Jewish Publication Society of America, 1959), pp. 311-12.

13.   J. Mélèze Modrzejewski, *The Jews of Egypt From Rameses II to Emperor Hadrian* (Edinburgh: T. & T. Clark, 1995), p. 164. On Jewish self-regulation in Alexandria see Strabo in Josephus, *Ant.* 14.114.

14.   Many modern scholars have assumed that the Jews of Alexandria formed an autonomous organization as a *politeuma*, whose existence as a quasi-civic body was resented by the Greeks deprived of their city council. On the Jewish *politeuma*, see especially A. Kasher, *The Jews in Hellenistic and Roman Egypt: The Struggle for Equal Rights* (Texte und Studien zum antiken Judentum, 7; Tübingen: J.C.B. Mohr [Paul Siebeck], 1985). This conception has been shown, however, to lack supporting evidence, see Mélèze Modrzejewski, *The Jews of Egypt*, p. 82; S. Honigman, 'The Birth of a Diaspora', in S.J.D. Cohen and E.S. Frerichs (eds.), *Diasporas in Antiquity* (Atlanta: Scholars Press, 1993), p. 93-128 (95); G. Lüderitz, 'What is the Politeuma?', in J. van Henten and P. van der Horst (eds.), *Studies in Early Jewish Epigraphy* (Leiden: E.J. Brill, 1994), pp. 183-225 (204-208).

15.   Lewis, *Life in Egypt*, Chapter 10.

claimed citizenship in the city. His writings indicate a relatively positive attitude towards Roman rule. Philo's account of the struggles under Flaccus ignores the role of opposition to Rome among lower-class Alexandrian Jews, whose existence is implied in Philo but is explicit in other sources.[16] Philo stresses Jewish loyalty to Rome, and supports Roman rule as that which, in the normal course of events, guarantees both Jewish rights and the social stability which benefits the pursuit of the contemplative life.[17]

While Philo is generally positive towards Roman rule and Greek culture—he avoids portraying Jews in conflict with Greeks,[18] and seeks to show the best of Hellenism to be compatible, if not identified, with Judaism—he is profoundly negative, with very little exception, about Egypt and the Egyptians. A review of Philo's attitude towards Egypt and Egyptians suggests that several important influences may have contributed to his hostile portrayal. The first is the heritage of a long history of negative views of Egypt and Egyptians in Jewish tradition. Though not wholly negative, many traditions emphasized especially the story of the persecution of the Hebrews in Moses' Egypt and their liberation from that land; the divine command not to follow 'after the doings of the land of Egypt';[19] the association of Egypt with sensuality and hedonism;[20] prophetic attacks looking forward to the destruction of Egypt's gods;[21] and the condemnation of Egyptian religion throughout Hellenistic Jewish writings, in particular the worship of deified animals, which offends against the fundamental principle of

16. See M. Pucci Ben Zeev, 'New Perspectives on the Jewish–Greek Hostilities in Alexandria During the Reign of Emperor Caligula', *JSJ* 21.2 (1990), pp. 227-35 (234). For Philo's evidence see J. Barclay, *Jews in the Mediterranean Diaspora From Alexander to Trajan (323 BCE–117 CE)* (Edinburgh: T. & T. Clark, 1996), pp. 54-57; on other evidence, see *CPJ* II.153, ll. 96-97; *CPJ* II.152; Josephus, *Ant.* 19.278-79.

17. See R. Barraclough, 'Philo's Politics: Roman Rule and Hellenistic Judaism', in *ANRW*, II.21.1, pp. 417-553 (449-75).

18. K. Goudriann, 'Ethnical Strategies in Graeco-Roman Egypt', in P. Bilde, T. Engberg-Pedersen, L. Hannestad and J. Zahle (eds.), *Ethnicity in Hellenistic Egypt* (Aarhus: Aarhus University Press, 1992), pp. 74-99 (82-85).

19. Lev. 18.3.

20. This is implied in stories of Egyptians lusting after Hebrews (Gen. 12; Gen. 39), and is most explicit in the coarse language of Ezekiel's denunciation of Israel's search for alliance with Egypt, 'your neighbours with the large members' (Ezek. 16.26); Josephus, *Ant.* 2.201.

21. Isa. 19.1, 3; Jer. 43.12-13; 46.25; Ezek. 20.7-9; 30.13 (MT).

monotheism.[22] All of these factors appear in Philo's hostile construction of both the Egyptians of Scripture and of his own time, and, as others have already observed, there is not always a clear distinction between biblical and contemporary Egypt in Philo's writing.[23] Furthermore, it is notable that in a number of respects Philo develops a sustained hostility towards Egyptians to a degree unprecedented in earlier Jewish writings.[24]

An important aspect of Philo's work, which he shares with other Graeco-Roman Jewish writers, such as Josephus, is his apologetic defence of Judaism against hostile traditions about the Jews. Many of these hostile accounts focused on pejorative constructions of the Hebrews in the Exodus story, and emphasized, among other things, the seditious nature of the Jews, their impiety, and their hostility to foreigners.[25] Manetho's *Aigyptiaka* is itself an apologetic work written as a defence of native Egyptian history. In its response to the negative portrayal of Egyptians in Jewish tradition, Manetho's history provides the earliest known account of the Exodus which is hostile to the Hebrews:[26] this alleges that the ancestors of the Jews planned to overthrow the government of Egypt and to exterminate the Egyptians,[27] and describes their impious attacks on Egyptian temples.[28] Traditions like these were later developed by polemical authors writing against the Jews in Philo's Alexandria. Most prominent here was Apion, a member of a rival Alexandrian embassy sent to Rome

22.   *Letter of Aristeas*, p. 138; *5 Sib. Or.*, pp. 279-80.

23.   See, for example, on Philo's portrayal of Joseph, M. Niehoff, *The Figure of Joseph in Post-Biblical Jewish Literature* (Leiden: E.J. Brill, 1992), p. 78.

24.   In contrast with, for example, the *Third Sibylline Oracle* which, while deeply hostile to idolatry and to other nations generally, contains no real signs of anti-Egyptian sentiment, see C. Holladay, 'Jewish Responses to Hellenistic Culture in Early Ptolemaic Egypt', in P. Bilde, T. Engberg-Pedersen, L. Hannestad and J. Zahle (eds.), *Ethnicity in Hellenistic Egypt*, pp. 139-63 (154-55).

25.   For the influence of such charges on Philo's attitude to Egyptians, see A. Mendelson, *Philo's Jewish Identity* (Atlanta: Scholars Press, 1988), pp. 117-22. Josephus claims that 'the libels upon us [Jews] originated with the Egyptians', referring especially to stories about the Exodus, and the opposition of Jewish cult to Egyptian animal worship (*Apion* 1.223-26). See generally, J. Gager, *The Origins of Anti-Semitism* (Oxford: Oxford University Press, 1985), pp. 40-54.

26.   See G. Sterling, *Historiography and Self-Definition* (Leiden: E.J. Brill, 1992), pp. 117-36.

27.   Josephus, *Apion* 1.81

28.   Josephus, *Apion* 1.75-76

alongside that of Philo, and whose activities are known from Josephus's *Contra Apionem*. It is likely that Philo was aware of the nature
of Apion's slurs against the Jews. Apion's propaganda seems to have
been aimed at undermining the notion that Jews could be citizens of
Alexandria. He stresses the Jews' non-Greek character by asserting
their Egyptian origin, and alleges that Jews are bound by an oath of
hostility to Greeks, exclaiming that Jewish refusal to participate in
other cults must exclude them from civic status.[29]

Philo's work responds at various levels to such allegations: he
stresses, for example, the philanthropy of Mosaic teaching to counter
the charge of Jewish misanthropy,[30] and, as a recent treatment of
Philo's *De Vita Mosis* suggests, he provides 'a rationale for Scripture's decidedly hostile view of the Egyptians'.[31] He is also keen to
show both the Hebrews of the past and the Jews of contemporary
Alexandria to be loyal and pious subjects. Against the identification of
the Hebrews/Jews with Egyptians, I will show below that he emphati-
cally distinguishes the Jews and their ancestors from the Egyptians.

Finally, Philo's comments on Egypt and the Egyptians situate him,
more than any other Jewish writer of antiquity, within the Graeco-
Roman tradition of contempt for Egyptians and their culture,[32] a
tradition rooted in outsiders' perceptions of Egypt, and not in the Hel-
lenic community of Egypt, which had embraced aspects of Egyptian
culture with enthusiasm. Before the establishment of the Hellenistic
kingdom of Egypt, Greek writers already represented an ambivalence
towards Egypt.[33] While many shared the favourable *topos* that idealized Egypt as the birthplace of Greek wisdom and law,[34] there also

29.   Josephus, *Apion* 2.65.
30.   E.g. *Spec. Leg.* 2.165-67.
31.   D. Sills, 'Vicious Rumors: Mosaic Narratives in First-Century Alexandria',
in E. Lovering (ed.), *SBLSP* 31; (Atlanta: Scholars Press, 1992), pp. 684-94 (694).
32.   It should not surprise that Reinhold's survey of Roman attitudes towards
Egypt places Philo's views alongside those of Juvenal and Tacitus, who represent
slightly later examples of extreme negative stereotyping of the Egyptians. See
M. Reinhold, 'Roman Attitudes Towards Egyptians', *The Ancient World* 3.3-4
(1980), pp. 97-103 (101).
33.   See K. Smelik and E. Hemelrijk, '"Who Knows What Monsters Demented
Egypt Worships?" Opinions on Egyptian Animal Worship in Antiquity as Part of
the Ancient Conception of Egypt', in *ANRW*, II.17.4, pp. 1852-2000 (1869-83,
esp. 1878).
34.   Herodotus, *Histories* 1.30; Plato, *Timaeus* 21E-25D (though here the

developed a most unfavourable conception of the Egyptians as profoundly non-Hellenic, expressed vividly in Aeschylus's portrayal of the Egyptians as barbarians without proper respect for Greeks, or Herodotus's description of Egyptian culture as a world in reverse, or the disparaging contrast of superstitious Egyptians with sober Greeks.[35] Egyptians were characterized as inhospitable to foreigners,[36] and as deceitful by nature.[37]

These themes were developed in foreign Graeco-Roman perspectives on Egypt in later periods, with a growing hostility towards Egyptian animal worship. By Philo's time, the negative stereotyping of Egyptians and, to an extent, Alexandrians, had received special impetus from Octavian's propaganda war against Cleopatra and Antony. This stressed the political untrustworthiness of Egyptians (making no distinction between Greek Egyptians such as Cleopatra and native Egyptians) seen as treacherous and seditious, and the low morality of the voluptuous Egyptians viewed as at odds with the sobriety of Roman values, especially exploiting Roman revulsion at Egyptian animal worship. Such a negative portrayal of Egyptians was designed to enhance Octavian's reputation as the saviour of the Roman world from the menace of the east in what was, primarily, a civil war.[38]

For Philo, the adoption of a strong anti-Egyptian attitude served to associate the Jews with the Hellenistic Roman world in their opposition to and otherness from native Egyptians. It expressed a sense of identification not only culturally but also politically with the ruling class of Roman Egypt.

Jewish Hellenistic attacks on Egyptian animal worship, which, in their Egyptian focus, have no obvious explicit basis in Scripture, may well have been intended to make the Jewish prohibition on idolatry attractive to non-Jews if they were already impressed by Greek philosophical objections to Egyptian theriomorphic religion.[39] But it is also

reputed superiority of Egyptian culture is qualified).

35.   Aeschylus, *Supplices*; Herodotus, *Histories* 2.91; Anaxandrides in Athenaeus, *Deipnosophistae* 7. 299F-300A.

36.   Plato, *Nomoi* 953E.

37.   Aristophanes, *Thesmophoriazusae* 922.

38.   On Octavian's propaganda see Smelik and Hemelrijk, '"Who Knows What Monsters"', pp. 1853-55, 1927-28. On Roman contempt for Egyptians see also Reinhold, 'Roman Attitudes Towards Egyptians'.

39.   For a positive Graeco-Roman view of Jewish rejection of Egyptian animal

clear that Jewish attacks on Egyptian animal worship could function as part of a polemic specific to the situation of Egypt, to identify the Jews as Hellenes in their contempt for animal worship, and to discredit their opponents by association with Egyptians.

The categorization of opponents as Egyptians was a strategy used by both sides in the conflict between Jews and their opponents in Alexandria in 38–41 CE. This strategy, as Goudriann suggests, was directly related to the problems for those of uncertain social status in Egypt, such as the Jews and rural Greeks, following Rome's reorganization of the province.[40] In this context, Philo implies by various means— including the accusation of Egyptian animal worship—the Egyptian identity of the Jews' opponents. Josephus's record of the crisis also counters Apion's polemical claim that Jews are to be identified as Egyptians and not as Alexandrian citizens by implying that Apion's attack on Jewish food laws is merely a front for his Egyptian reverence for animals, showing his non-Hellenic origins and unsuitability for Alexandrian citizenship.[41] Josephus explicitly alleges that Apion concealed his Egyptian origins in order to appear to be an authentic Alexandrian.[42] We see a similar underlying strategy at work (though without reference to animal worship) in the accusation of Isidorus, one of the chief Alexandrian opponents of the Jews: in the account of his trial at Rome he is made to accuse the Jews

> ...of wishing to stir up the whole world...They do not think the same way as the Alexandrians, but more like Egyptians.[43]

Goudriann's more detailed analysis of this question shows clearly the purpose of this 'ethnic strategy':

> Both parties tried to associate themselves as much as possible with the Hellenic ethnic entity and claimed to be real Alexandrians, with the exclusion of the other; both parties kept the Egyptians at the largest possible distance and tried to push down the adversaries to that level.[44]

worship, see Strabo, 16.2.35-36; Smelik and Hemelrijk, '"Who Knows What Monsters"', p. 1919.
40.   Goudriann, 'Ethnical Strategies', pp. 86-94.
41.   Josephus, *Apion* 2.137-41.
42.   Josephus, *Apion* 2.28-29.
43.   *Acta Isidori*, Recension C Col. 2, ll. 20-26 in H. Musurillo (ed.), *The Acts of the Pagan Martyrs: Acta Alexandrinorum* (Oxford: Clarendon Press, 1954), p. 23.
44.   Goudriann, 'Ethnical Strategies', p. 88.

Philo on Egypt and Egyptians

In the light of this sketch of Philo's local situation and the likely influences surrounding his construction of Egypt and the Egyptians, the substance of Philo's attitudes should be considered in greater detail. By way of a preliminary observation, Philo's works appear to include a few examples of a more neutral or even positive attitude towards things Egyptian. On closer inspection, however, these do not provide evidence for a more positive attitude on Philo's part.

In the first case, Eusebius cites Philo in a description of Egyptian devotion to the crocodile, which lives in 'the most sacred Nile (ἐν τῷ ἱερωτάτῳ Νείλῳ)', without condemning—in contrast to Philo's emphatic denunciations elsewhere—those who honour the river.[45] The superlative ἱερώτατος is, however, probably a fourth-century addition. Among the various titles of reverence used of the Nile, ἱερώτατος is not otherwise attested before the reign of Hadrian, and has a particular association with imperial power.[46] It is very probable, in view of Philo's ideology and the history of ἱερώτατος as a title of the Nile, that the 'most sacred Nile' mentioned here is, as Bonneau argues, a projection of Eusebius, in view of the long established usage of the expression since the time of Hadrian.[47]

In a second case, the Egyptians are mentioned favourably in Philo's preface to his treatment of the Decalogue in his *Special Laws*: here, in order to counter ridicule of the practice of circumcision, Philo appeals to the fact that it is practised by other peoples, and 'particularly by the Egyptians, a people regarded as preeminent for its populousness, its antiquity and its attachment to philosophy'.[48] Admiration of the antiquity and ancient wisdom of the Egyptians is a *topos* in Graeco-Roman writings on Egypt, sometimes in contexts which also attack other aspects of Egyptian culture. Philo's statement should be seen in a

---

45.   Eusebius, *PE* VII.13, citing Philo, *De Providentia* 2.65.

46.   A recent study states that 'ἱερώτατος ne s'emploie pas sans discernement; il ne concerne que l'empereur, son entourage et ce qui relève exclusivement du pouvoir impérial: le fisc et le Nil', cf. D. Bonneau, 'La divinité du Nil sous le principat en Egypte', *ANRW*, II.18.5, pp. 3195-215 (3201).

47.   Bonneau, 'La divinité du Nil', pp. 3201-2.

48.   *Spec. Leg.* 1.3.

similar light, and specifically as the exploitation of a commonplace for apologetic purposes.[49]

Much of what Philo says about Egypt belongs to his commentaries on the Pentateuch, devoted to the interpretation—mostly by means of allegory—of the Pentateuch as the source of the highest wisdom. What he has to say here is, for the most part, negative. He draws out three main symbolic understandings of Egypt, which frequently occur together: Egypt is (1) the body, (2) αἴσθησις, or sense, (3) πάθος, or passion.

This symbolic interpretation is bound up with Philo's dualistic conception of human being: developing Platonic teaching he associates the body with the earth and irrational passions, and the mind with the divine realm and reason, and portrays the soul as the bridge between body and mind. Philo's interpretation is also dominated by the contrast between knowledge which is derived purely from senseperceived speculation, which is imperfect, and that wisdom which is identified with the mystic experience of the vision of God. Nevertheless, the 'lower' form of learning functions in the preparation of the soul for its higher destination.

Various aspects of these conceptions are read out of the pentateuchal narratives of the migrations of the ancestors: the lands visited prior to settlement in the land of Canaan—among which Egypt is central—symbolize stages in the soul's journey away from the body, the passions, and imperfect knowledge based on sense-perception, and towards the promised homeland of the heavenly realm, identified with the land of wisdom, virtue, or the knowledge of God.[50]

In Philo's interpretation of the Pentateuch, the Egypt of the ancestors before Moses is predominantly a symbol of the body, the sphere of sense-perceptions and passions, a place where the wise are only sojourners on the journey towards virtue.[51] It is possible that the symbolic interpretation of Egypt as the body was part of a wider tradition

49.   So S. Daniel, *De Specialibus Legibus I et II* (Paris: Cerf, 1975), p. 13 n. 4. Similarly, the instruction of the young Moses by learned Egyptians (*Vit. Mos.* 1.23-24) may reflect the tradition in Plato's *Laws* that mathematics and music are central to Egyptian learning, see F. Colson, *Philo* (Cambridge, MA: Harvard University Press; London: Heinemann, 1984), *VI*, pp. 286-87.

50.   *Rer. Div. Her.* 293, 314.

51.   See P. Qarni, 'Biblical Egypt as a Symbol in Philo's Allegory', *Shnaton* 5-6 (1982), pp. 197-204 (198) (Hebrew).

mentioned by Philo;[52] the representation of Egypt as a voluptuous, hedonistic land in Jewish and non-Jewish Graeco-Roman writings may have lent support to the identification of Egypt as the land of the body.

Abraham's sojourn in Egypt represents the soul's encounter with and departure from that imperfect knowledge acquired by the body, sense-perceived knowledge, exemplified by the figure of Hagar.[53] Isaac, who represents the perfected person, freed from the passions, was commanded not to go down into Egypt, which, Philo, reflecting a play on the resemblance between מצרים(Egypt) and מצורים (oppressing), connects with the oppression of the mind by the passions.[54]

The figure of Joseph who remained in Egypt portrays the compromising or 'mixed' soul: his place between the Egyptians and his family at his father's funeral shows that

> his object is to be equally in touch with the concerns of the body, which is
> Egypt, and those of the soul which are kept as in a treasury in his father's
> house.[55]

Although champion of the bodily sphere, Joseph did not attain to the much superior treasure of the soul, because he did not abandon Egypt;[56] the transfer of his bones to Canaan at the time of the Exodus represents the removal of that part of him which remained uncorrupted, which did not belong to the land of the body.[57] Elaborating Jacob's reservations about going to Egypt, Philo portrays Egypt as a place which the wise should fear to enter because of its corrupting influences—especially idolatry—on the ancestral teachings.[58]

The identification of Egypt and the Egyptians with the realm of the body dominates Philo's allegorical interpretation of the Exodus as the liberation and migration of the soul from the sphere of the body and the passions.[59] The Passover celebrates the crossing from passion;[60] it

---

52. *Jos.* 151.
53. *Congr.* 20; *Quaest. in Gen.* 3.19.
54. *Quaest. in Gen.* 4.177; cf. L.L. Grabbe, *Etymology in Early Jewish Interpretation: The Hebrew Names in Philo* (Atlanta: Scholars Press, 1988), p. 130.
55. *Migr. Abr.* 160.
56. *Sobr.* 13.
57. *Migr. Abr.* 17-19.
58. *Jos.* 254.
59. *Abr.* 103; *Rer. Div. Her.* 255; *Somn.* 2.279; *Migr. Abr.* 151.
60. *Rer. Div. Her.* 255.

is a symbol of a change to a better state, from ignorance to wisdom.[61] In places it is made clear that the Egyptians represent unacceptable forms of philosophy—the rejection of Providence,[62] or the Epicurean doctrine that pleasure is the highest good.[63]

While Philo follows Scripture in condemning various forms of idolatry, his writings reveal a special focus of hostility towards what he portrays as Egyptian idolatry. Perhaps following earlier Jewish tradition, Philo portrays the plagues as punishment for Egyptian idolatry:[64] the water of Egypt is polluted to punish the Egyptians for their reverence of water 'as the original source of the creation of the All'.[65] Moreover his interpretation of the Pentateuch shows a concern to avoid the implication that the Hebrews were themselves responsible for idolatrous or blasphemous activities after the Exodus time. According to Philo, the danger of idolatry continues in the journey away from Egypt because of Egyptian influence, which Philo connects with the 'mixed' nature of the emigrants who are mentioned briefly in Exod. 12.38, and whom he takes to have included Egyptians.[66] The worship of the Golden Calf is specifically identified as an instance of following the foolishness of Egyptian worship, though the biblical narrative of Exodus 32 does not make this identification.[67] The story of Israel's idolatry immediately following the revelation at Sinai was a great source of embarrassment in Jewish tradition.[68] Unlike Josephus, who omits the story of the Golden Calf altogether, Philo refers to the event several times, but, in an apparently unprecedented interpretation, he seeks to divert the blame from the Hebrews by attributing this example of animal-centred idolatry to Egyptian influence.

Philo makes a similar point in his portrayal of the blasphemer of

61.   *Quaest. in Ex.* 1.4.
62.   *Quaest. in Gen.* 4.87.
63.   *Fug.* 148.
64.   See *Wis.* 11.15-20; 12.23-27; 15.18-16.1.
65.   *Vit. Mos.* 1.98.
66.   *Vit. Mos.* 1.147.
67.   *Vit. Mos.* 2.161-2; *Fug.* 90; *Ebr.* 95; *Spec. Leg.* 1.79; 3.125. The worship of the Golden Calf was apparently identified with the veneration of Apis, so F. Colson and G. Whittaker, *Philo* (Cambridge, MA: Harvard University Press, 1988), III, p. 503 (§95).
68.   See M. Aberbach and L. Smolar, 'The Golden Calf Episode in Postbiblical Literature', *HUCA* 39 (1968), pp. 91-116.

Lev. 24.10-23.[69] This figure is described in Leviticus 24 as the son of an Israelite woman, a fact repeated three times, and of an Egyptian father, a point made only once (Lev. 24.10) and not made to explain the man's offence. Philo, however, connects the man's blasphemy precisely with his Egyptian origins: in this interpretation the blasphemer denied the ancestral customs (τῶν πατρίων ἐθῶν) of his mother, and turned to the Egyptian impiety (ἀσέβεια), having embraced the atheism (ἀθεότης) of these people. This is followed by a general condemnation of the Egyptian 'atheism' which reverences the earth above heaven, and the Nile as a god.[70]

As we have already seen, a striking aspect of Philo's polemic against contemporary opponents of the Jews in Alexandria is to suggest their Egyptian identity, partly by associating them with Egyptian idolatry, despite the fact that the chief opponents clearly belonged to the citizen-body of Alexandria.[71] In Philo's *Legatio* the Jews' Alexandrian opponents are also identified as animal-worshipping idolaters in order to portray them, in contrast to the Jews, as impious. The *Legatio* insists controversially on linking attacks on Alexandria's Jewish prayer-houses, in which images of the Emperor Gaius were installed, with Gaius's self-deification.[72] According to this view, Gaius's hostility towards the Jews was manipulated by their enemies, who persuaded him of his divine status and of the Jews' impiety in refusing to honour him as a god.[73] Philo responds by arguing that the opponents in fact showed their impiety towards the Emperor by depriving the Jews of their legitimate means of honouring him in their prayer-houses. Instead, he emphasizes the godlessness of the Alexandrian opponents, whose piety towards Gaius is condemned as inauthentic, and who are identified as idolatrous and godless Egyptians; it is this godlessness, according to Philo, which made them and their city ideal

69.   *Vit. Mos.* 2.192-208.

70.   *Vit. Mos.* 2.194-95.

71.   The opponents who insulted the visiting Jewish king, Agrippa I, were members of the gymnasium and therefore citizens of the Greek city of Alexandria, see *Flacc.* 34. On Philo's identification of the opponents as Egyptians, see the recent study by Goudriann, 'Ethnical Strategies', pp. 87-89.

72.   Smallwood argues that Philo manipulated the chronology of events in order to achieve this link, since Gaius did not claim divinity prior to the attacks on the prayer-houses. E.M. Smallwood, *Philonis Alexandrini Legatio ad Gaium* (Leiden: E.J. Brill, 1979), pp. 3, 207.

73.   *Leg. Gai.* 115-20.

as the centre of the deification of Gaius.[74]

If Philo's attack on Egyptian idolatry is to be explained as a reaction against the attraction of some contemporary Jews to the Egyptian cults of Alexandria, it must be said that we have no good evidence for such attractions having taken place in Philo's time. On the other hand, Philo's attacks on Egyptians/Alexandrians as idolatrous and blasphemous, and his repeated emphasis on their animal worship, can be seen to serve two main functions. First, he avoids implicating the Hebrews in responsibility for idolatrous or blasphemous actions by transferring the blame explicitly to Egyptian sources, so reinforcing the idea that authentic Judaism has nothing to do with animal-worshipping Egyptians; in this he may well have deliberately intended that Jewish rejection of Egyptian animal worship be seen as allied with Graeco-Roman abhorrence at this practice.[75] Secondly, the attack on the Alexandrian opponents as godless Egyptians serves to deflect onto them the charge of Jewish godlessness which was made by the opponents, in relation to Jewish refusal to participate in the imperial cult, onto the opponents themselves. Perhaps even more importantly in the context of the controversy over citizenship in Alexandria, Philo discredits his Alexandrian opponents by associating them, as Egyptians, with that group which was especially held in contempt by Rome, whose policies confined them to low status and lack of citizenship rights.

From the beginning of his account of the crisis in *In Flaccum*, Philo identifies the cause of the troubles with the seditious character of the Egyptians.[76] This theme is elaborated in Philo's description of the

74.   *Leg. Gai.* 162-63. *Leg. Gai.* 138-39 describes the ancestors of the Alexandrians under the Ptolemies as those who venerated wild animals and who were therefore naturally suited to venerate the Ptolemies as gods. On Gaius's belief that the city had originated the idea of his divinity, see *Leg. Gai.* 338.

75.   D. Zeller, 'Das Verhältnis', p. 79.

76.   *Flacc.* 17. Pelletier notes in relation to this passage that the seditious nature of contemporary Egyptians may also be suggested by the story of the attempted rebellion led by an Egyptian, recorded by Josephus (*War* 2.261-3; *Ant.* 20.171) and Acts 21.37-9, cf. A. Pelletier, *In Flaccum* (Paris: Cerf, 1967), p. 170. The Egyptian mentioned here, however, is presumably a Jew, cf. E. Schürer, *The History of the Jewish People in the Age of Jesus Christ* (rev. ed. G. Vermes, F. Millar and M. Black; Edinburgh: T. & T. Clark, 1973), I, p. 464.

Alexandrians' deception of Flaccus and Gaius,[77] and of the Alexandrians' preparations for rebellion, which he contrasts with the loyalty of the Jews of Alexandria to Rome.[78] Alexandrian hostility towards the visiting Jewish king, Agrippa I, stems from the slanderous nature of the Egyptians—βάσκανον γὰρ φύσει τὸ Αἰγυπτιακόν[79]—exemplified by one of the leading opponents, Isidorus, who is later condemned by the leading citizens as βασκαίνων.[80] The Egyptian nature of the opponents is also implied in the claim which directly relates their antagonism to ancient Egyptian hatred of the Jews.[81] Philo's reply to those who attempt to deprive the Jews (or perhaps some Jews) of their former social status is to denigrate the status of the accusers, and to imply that they, and not the Jews whom Philo represents, were not authentic citizens of Alexandria.[82] Philo's opponents are also portrayed in ways that appeal to aspects of the negative Roman stereotype of Egyptians as seditious, arrogant, anti-Roman, animal worshippers. The message is clear: it is the Jewish community and not that of their opponents which is loyal to Rome; the enemies of the Jews are those whom the Hellenistic Roman world rejects.

An important example of Philo's contrast between the Jews and the Egyptians is to do with the treatment of strangers. Philo's emphasis on the great justice with which Jewish tradition treats strangers or foreigners may partly reflect an apologetic defence against allegations of Jewish misanthropy. His attack on Egyptian inhospitality towards strangers may serve part of that purpose, but it is also likely that he

77.   *Leg. Gai.* 166.

78.   See, for example, *Flacc.* 48-52 (Alexandrian Jews honour Rome in their prayer-houses); 56 (Alexandrian Jews mourn Drusilla); 86-94 (Alexandrian Jews have no stockpile of weapons).

79.   *Flacc.* 29.

80.   *Flacc.* 143. The same connection underlies Philo's denunciation of the Egyptians in *Agr.* 62-64: there, Pharaoh's questioning of Joseph's brothers (Gen. 47.3) is associated with one who is βάσκανος.

81.   Josephus or his source records that libels against the Jews originated with the Egyptians and that these began with 'the original grievance of the domination of our ancestors over their country' (that is, in the time of Joseph), see Josephus, *Apion* 1.223-4. The Egyptian cult of animals is also cited as a source of conflict here, on account of Egyptian envy of the success of Judaism in attracting admirers (*Apion* 1.225-6).

82.   See S. McKnight, *A Light among the Gentiles: Jewish Missionary Activity in the Second Temple Period* (Minneapolis: Fortress Press, 1991), p. 130 n. 62.

intended deliberately to denigrate the Egyptians in terms which would make a strong impact on a Hellenistic audience.

Philo is keen to stress the injustice and inhumanity of the Egyptians of the Exodus time, in contrast to the virtues of the Hebrews. The most positive of Mosaic teachings on the Egyptians receives a partly negative focus in Philo's interpretation. The Deuteronomic command, 'Thou shalt not abhor an Egyptian, because thou wast a stranger in his land' (Deut. 23.7) is made to show that Moses requires settlers (μέτοικοι) to go beyond the ordinary standards of fairness: they are to show no malice 'to those whose hospitality to strangers is followed by maltreatment', noting with strong emphasis the Egyptians' injustice towards the Hebrews.[83]

Philo's *De Vita Mosis* presents Moses as the ideal wise hero in terms that appeal strongly to aspects of Greek tradition. By contrast the Pharaoh of the Exodus in this work is shown as an example of the utterly unjust ruler who flouts the sacred duties of rulers according to both Greek and Jewish standards. His enslavement of the Hebrews is a betrayal of the ruler's duties towards guest-strangers (ξένοι) who should be treated as 'suppliants' (ἱκέται), privileged residents (μέτοικοι) and friends (φίλοι)

> who are anxious to obtain equal rights with the burgesses and are near to being citizens because they differ little from the original inhabitants.[84]

Wolfson and others have seen a reference here to the struggle over the civic status of Jews in Philo's Alexandria.[85] This seems improbable, however, in view of the designation of 'the Jews' of the Exodus period either as ξένοι, a status Philo explicitly rejects in the context of the Alexandrian crisis, or as little different from the native Egyptians.[86] Philo's emphasis here is rather on the proper treatment of ξένοι as 'guest-strangers'.[87] Pharaoh fails the divine laws of Moses which demand proper treatment of the stranger.[88] But he also fails by Greek

83.   *Virt.* 105-108. See also *Quaest. in Exod.* 2.2.
84.   *Vit. Mos.* 1.34-6.
85.   H. Wolfson, *Philo: Foundations of Religious Philosophy in Judaism, Christianity and Islam* (Cambridge, MA: Harvard University Press, 1947), II, pp. 398-99.
86.   Barraclough, 'Philo's Politics' (p. 239, Kasher's identification of the *autochthonoi* as the upper-class is not justified by Philo's usage), p. 426.
87.   As, clearly, in *Vit. Mos.* 1.275.
88.   Exod. 23.9; Lev. 19.34; Deut. 10.19.

standards of justice in which the protection of the 'suppliant' was a sacred duty.[89] Perhaps Philo was thinking here particularly of Aeschylus's *Supplices* who, as ξένοι and ἱκέται, fleeing from the 'wanton men of Aegyptus' (who are portrayed most unfavourably), receive the protection of the king of Argos, as required by Zeus, god of the stranger and suppliant.[90] What the Argives offer the 'suppliants' is strikingly like what, in Philo's view, was required of Pharaoh:

> That we be settlers in this land (μετοικεῖν), be free (ἐλευθέρους), subject to no seizure, and secure from robbery of man; that no one, native or alien, carry us captive... any landholder who refuses to rescue us should both forfeit his rights and suffer public banishment.[91]

It is interesting to speculate that Philo might deliberately allude in *Vit. Mos.* 1.34-36, therefore, to a Greek work and tradition which is already hostile towards Egypt as part of his portrayal of Pharaoh as the unjust ruler.

Philo brings to the Exodus narratives a strong emphasis on the distinction between Egyptian and Hebrew. He underlines Moses' status as a Chaldaean or Hebrew, distinct from the Egyptians, in the preface to his account of Moses' birth where he is 'a Chaldaean'.[92] Philo emphasizes the error of the daughters of the priest of Midian who thought Moses was an Egyptian, though the point is not corrected in Exod. 2.19.[93] As the adopted grandson of Pharaoh, Moses is shown to have been loyal to his adopted family—perhaps responding to the charge that Moses betrayed his Egyptian benefactors—until, that is, the persecution of Pharaoh forced him to reject his Egyptian family;[94] at the same time, it is made clear that Moses was always loyal to his natural family and 'zealous for the discipline and culture of his kinsmen and ancestors'.[95] Philo's portrait of Moses firmly rejects any notion, such

89. On Pharaoh's treatment of the Hebrews as 'sacrilegous', see V. Nikiprowetzky, 'Les Suppliants Chez Philon d'Alexandrie', *REJ* 4.2.122 (1963), pp. 241-378 (250).

90. Aeschylus, *Supplices,* lines 347, 360, 478-79.

91. Aeschylus, *Suppliant Maidens* (ed. H. Weir Smyth, *Aeschylus* [London: Heinemann, 1922]), I, lines 606-14.

92. *Vit. Mos.* 1.5 (many manuscripts read ἑβραῖος here instead; the words are often equivalent in Philo's usage); see also *Mut. Nom.* 118.

93. *Mut. Nom.* 118.

94. *Vit. Mos.* 1.149-50.

95. *Vit. Mos.* 1.32.

as one finds in Manetho, that Moses was an Egyptian. The greatest representative of Jewish tradition is shown, in terms stronger than those of Scripture, to have been utterly distinct from the Egyptians.

Philo on Alexandria

In the second part of this paper I consider briefly the question of Philo's identification with Alexandria. What is (perhaps) the most important question regarding Philo's local allegiances is one that cannot be answered with certainty: that is, whether he identified as a citizen of Alexandria, or, as Kasher argues, only as a 'citizen' of the local Jewish community organization.[96] The much discussed question of the Jews and Alexandrian citizenship in Philo's time is not one that can be rehearsed here in detail. Most scholars assume, however, on the basis of his social relations and education that Philo was one of few Jews who did enjoy citizenship of the city. Philo's writings suggest that an important part of his representations in Rome, following attacks on the Jews of Alexandria in CE 38, was to defend the interests of Jews who regarded themselves as citizens.[97] The evidence of his Alexandrian opponents, whether in the papyri or as preserved by Josephus, together with the imperial decree of Claudius, also indicates that an important part of the dispute in which Philo was involved concerned the Alexandrian citizenship of some Jews.[98]

Philo speaks more broadly of Jewish local allegiances in the context of attacks on the Alexandrian Jews from CE 38. Here he describes the conspiracy of the Roman prefect Flaccus, the creature of a small faction of Alexandrians,[99] responsible for attacks on the Jewish prayer-houses of Alexandria, and for a decree that deprived the Jews of certain rights, which Philo expresses in terms of a reduction in status to that of 'foreigners and aliens', that is, with no right of permanent

96. Kasher, *The Jews*, p. 238.
97. See the recent discussion by Barclay, *Jews*, pp. 66-71 who suggests that Philo's complaint over the method of scourging the leaders of the Jewish community may reflect that they, but not all Jews, were entitled to be scourged according to the practice for citizens (*Flacc.* 78-80), and that the sending of a second embassy after Philo's may suggest that some Jews saw Philo's embassy as too much concerned with defending their narrow interests as citizens.
98. See above, pp. 81-82.
99. See *Flacc.* 23.

residence in the city.[100] Philo's *In Flaccum* emphasizes, immediately subsequent to Flaccus's decree, the expulsion of Jews from all parts of the city and their enforced confinement in 'a very small part of one'[101]—robbed of their homes and property, and liable to fatal violence when found outside the newly imposed 'Jewish' quarter.[102] In spite of the difficulties surrounding the interpretation of the Jewish rights at the centre of the controversy, Philo clearly expresses outrage at the attempt to disassociate or dislodge the Jews from the city of Alexandria—or most of it[103]—the situation in which 'the city was no longer their "own homeland", their *idia*; they could now be displaced at will'.[104] It is the sense of the Jews' homelessness that is emphasized in both Philo's *In Flaccum* and the *Legatio*. Flaccus' edict and the actions of the Alexandrian opponents which accompanied it made the Jews 'hearthless and homeless, outcasts and exiles from their own houses (καὶ ἀνοίκους καὶ ἀνεστίους, ἐξεωσμένους καὶ πεφυγαδευμένους τῶν ἰδίων οἴκων)'.[105] This is the first point made about their condition in the Jews' prayer of thanksgiving on the beach at Alexandria following Flaccus' arrest:

> Most mighty king of mortals and immortals, we have come here to call on earth and sea, and air and heaven... and on the whole world, to give Thee thanks. They are our only habitation, expelled as we are from all that men have wrought, robbed of our city and the buildings within its walls, public and private, alone of all men under the sun bereft of home and country (ἀπόλιδες καὶ ἀνέστοι) through the malignancy of a governor...[106]

The idea that Flaccus brought about the loss of the Alexandrian Jews' home is clear also in Philo's depiction of the fate of Flaccus, in which, to illustrate the working of Providence, the former prefect suffers

100.   *Flacc.* 53-54; 172. The Jews' reduced status is described in terms (ξένος, ἐπηλυς, ἀτιμία) which Philo often employs to refer to a social status distinctly contrasting with that of a citizen (*Cher.* 121; *Poster C.* 109; *Spec. Leg.* 4.70) or the loss of civic rights (*Spec. Leg.* 3.168).

101.   *Flacc.* 53-54.

102.   *Flacc.* 56-72.

103.   The implication of the attacks following Flaccus's edict is that as 'foreigners' (*Flacc.* 54) the Jews now had the right of domicile in one section only of Alexandria, see Smallwood, *Philonis Alexandrini*, p. 20.

104.   Mélèze Modrzejewski, *The Jews of Egypt*, p. 169.

105.   *Leg. Gai.* 123.

106.   *Flacc.* 123.

punishments which match his crimes against the Jews. These include Flaccus's arrest at a banquet, where

> ...it was only right that a hospitable hearth should be the scene where justice first fell on one who had destroyed numberless hearths and homes of persons that had done no wrong.[107]

and his condition of exile from his *patris*.[108] This conception of the end of Flaccus underlines Philo's notion that the prefect had (temporarily) deprived Alexandrian Jews of their *patris*.

The relative significance of Philo's fight to 'show that we are Alexandrians', however, is made clear in his account of his embassy to Rome. News of the imminent desecration of the Temple, received by Philo at Puteoli, is imagined as something which threatens the existence of all Jews:

> For it is to be feared that the overthrow of the Temple will be accompanied by an order for the annihilation of our common name and nation from the man who deals in revolution on so great a scale.[109]

We should note that Philo does not state here in any straightforward way that problems affecting Jerusalem, or 'the Holy Land', should take precedence over the concerns of Jews elsewhere. His point is that Gaius's proposed attack on the Temple, like the attacks on Jewish institutions in Alexandria,[110] is a signal of a much more widespread threat to the Jewish world, so that local concerns must give way to the needs of 'a more universal interest, the corporate body of the Jews'.[111] That threat is additional to, and a necessary accompaniment of, the desecration of the Jerusalem Temple, and not simply to be identified with it.[112] Similarly, the view that the attack on the Jerusalem Temple is likely to be accompanied by danger to Jews everywhere is attributed to Agrippa I at the time of his protest to Gaius over the Jerusalem Temple. Just as Philo stated that it was no longer proper to attend exclusively to the problems of Alexandrian Jews, so here Agrippa is made to reflect that the attack on his *patris*, Jersualem, must be seen in

---

107. *Flacc.* 115.
108. *Flacc.* 158-59, 172.
109. *Leg. Gai.* 194.
110. *Leg. Gai.* 371.
111. *Leg. Gai.* 194.
112. Contra, for example, A. Pelletier, *Legatio ad Gaium* (Paris: Cerf, 1972), p. 204 n. 3.

wider perspective as accompanied by a threat to all Jews:

> For the danger which had fallen upon him was no trifle but one which
> involved the expulsion, enslavement, and wholesale spoliation of the
> Jews who dwelt not only in the Holy Land but everywhere through the
> habitable world.[113]

Philo's statements here reflect a strong sense that an attack on Jews in prominent centres, whether Alexandria or Jerusalem, will provide a model which will be readily imitated in other parts of the world.

When we consider the more general context of Philo's writings, there is a certain tension as regards the significance of homeland (*patris*). His discussions about the journey towards wisdom stress that the wise person, exemplified by Abraham (Gen. 12.1),[114] should abandon the homeland, often explicitly identified with ignorance or false religion,[115] in favour of the true homeland, that is the realm of God, or virtue.[116] Abandonment of homeland symbolizes, therefore, the first stage in the development of wisdom. Detachment from a particular homeland also forms a part in Philo's presentation of the wise as 'world-citizens' who transcend attachment to particular places:[117] here Philo develops early Stoic conceptions of the world as a city in which the wise share common citizenship.[118]

It would not be true to infer, however, that Philo's thought has no place for a more positive assessment of the significance of homeland. Patriotic devotion is for Philo, as for some other Jewish writers of the Hellenistic period,[119] among the highest goods and demanded by

113. *Leg. Gai.* 330.
114. *Praem. Poen.* 17; *Abr.* 67. The example of Abraham in this regard is followed exactly by the Therapeutae, cf. *Contempl.* 22.
115. *Spec. Leg.* 1.51-53.
116. *Conf. Ling.* 81; *Rer. Div. Her.* 26-27, 82; *Quaest. in Gen.* 4.74; *Agr.* 64-65; *Quaest. in Gen.* 4.178.
117. For the wise, every land is *patris* (*Prob.* 145); *Conf. Ling.* 106; *Somn.* 1.39.
118. On Zeno's Republic of the wise see *SVF* 1.262; cf. also *SVF* 3.322. For later Roman development of the citizenship of the *kosmos*, see Cicero, *De Legibus* 1.2.3. 61; Seneca, *Ad Marcian* 18.1. For discussion, see L. Storoni Mazzolani, *The Idea of the City in Roman Thought* (London: Hollis & Carter, 1970), pp. 35-37, 78-79. For Philo's views on ideal citizenship see Barraclough, 'Philo's Politics', pp. 538-42.
119. *Letter of Aristeas*; 2 Maccabees; cf. A. Kasher, 'Jerusalem as a "Metropo-

divine commandment in the Law of Moses.[120] Love of homeland,
according to Philo, is an almost universal condition of human experience:[121] patriotism is a sentiment common to noble Romans and Jews
according to the propaganda of Philo's version of Agrippa I's appeal
to Gaius on behalf of his own *patris*, Jerusalem;[122] and banishment is
portrayed as a penalty far worse than death.[123]

The *patris* in Philo's writings is, above all, one's place of birth and
education.[124] Like other Egyptian Jews of the Hellenistic-Roman
period, Philo refers explicitly to his city as his *patris*, albeit in passing.[125] Philo assumes a common sense of emotional attachment to local
homelands when he portrays pilgrimage to the Jerusalem Temple as
constituting 'the severest test', which requires temporary abandonment
of *patris* and family for life in a strange land (ξενιτεύειν).[126] There
is no doubt that devotion to the Temple and its laws is central to
Philo's Jewish identity. This does not mean, however, that his expression of that commitment should be read in terms which marginalize
his local allegiances. This issue is particularly important in relation to
Philo's representation of the crisis for Alexandrian Jews in 38 CE.

Contemplating the spread of attacks against Diaspora Jews after the
example of the treatment of the Alexandrian prayer-houses, Philo
explains that while such Jews hold Jerusalem as the Temple city to be
their 'mother city'

> ...yet those which are theirs by inheritance from their fathers, grand-
> fathers, and ancestors even farther back, are in each case accounted by

---

lis" in Philo's National Consciousness', *Cathedra* 11 (1979), pp. 45-56 (47).

120. *Mut. Nom.* 40; *Ebr.* 17; *Fug.* 29; *Virt.* 3; for condemnation of those who
refuse to defend the *patris*, see *Deus Imm.* 17-19; *Ebr.* 17.

121. *Abr.* 63; *Migr. Abr.* 217; *Spec. Leg.* 4.16-17.

122. *Leg. Gai.* 277-78; cf. Kasher, 'Jerusalem', p. 47.

123. *Abr.* 62-64; cf. Kasher, 'Jerusalem', pp. 45-46.

124. *Flacc.* 46, 158; *Vit. Cont.* 18. For colonists treating their land of adoption
rather than their mother city as *patris*, see *Conf. Ling.* 77-78.

125. *Leg. All.* 2.85; see also, for examples of Jewish references to a *patris* in
Egypt, Helenos (*CPJ* 2.151); *CII* 2.1530; W. Horbury and D. Noy (eds.), *Jewish
Inscriptions of Graeco-Roman Egypt* (Cambridge: Cambridge University Press,
1992), no. 38 (Leontopolis; probably Jewish).

126. *Spec. Leg.* 1.68. See further, Y. Amir, 'Philo's Version of the Pilgrimage
to Jerusalem' [Hebrew], in A. Oppenheimer, U. Rappaport and M. Stern (eds.),
Jerusalem in the Second Temple Period: Abraham Schalit Memorial Volume
(Jerusalem: Yad Izhak Beu-Zvi, 1980), pp. 154-65.

them to be their fatherland (*patris*) in which they were born and reared, while to some of them they have come at the time of their foundation as immigrants to the satisfaction of the founders.[127]

Kasher has argued that Philo here portrays Diaspora Jews' attachment to their *politeumata*—or independent community organizations—described as colonies, which are portrayed as secondary homelands in contrast to the genuine homeland which is Jerusalem.[128] It should be noted, however, that here Philo speaks of different conceptualizations of Jewish attachment to Diaspora homelands, and not exclusively in terms of colonization. Moreover, the context of Philo's statement shows that he does not portray Jerusalem as being of greater significance than the *patris*, but rather emphasizes the widespread phenomenon of Jews who feel rooted in other lands where, as in Alexandria, they are prepared to defend their institutions to the point of death.[129]

Philo was not alone among Jews in expressing a sense of pride in his association with Alexandria. Writing probably in the Ptolemaic period, Pseudo-Aristeas boasted that Alexandria 'surpasses all cities in size and prosperity'.[130] Similarly, Philo's pride in the city under Rome stresses the great benefactions of Augustus, whose monuments 'particularly in our own Alexandria' surpass the greatest works existing in other cities.[131] The importance of Alexandria as a great city in Philo's consciousness is also revealed, as David Runia has shown, in his comparison of the intelligible cosmos, the model for the material cosmos, with the foundation of Alexandria.[132]

Praise of the city is also found on the lips of two characters condemned by Philo for their role in attacks on the Jews of Alexandria in his own time. Flaccus, former governor of Egypt, laments his

127. *Flacc.* 46. For the *patris* as the place of birth and education see also *Vit. Cont.* 18; *Flacc.* 158.

128. Kasher, *The Jews*, pp. 236-38.

129. *Flacc.* 48.

130. *Letter of Aristeas* 109, see G. Sterling, '"Thus are Israel": Jewish Self-Definition in Alexandria', *The Studia Philonica Annual* 7 (1995), pp. 1-18 (9).

131. *Leg. Gai.* 150.

132. D. Runia, 'Polis and Megalopolis: Philo and the Founding of Alexandria', *Mnemosyne* 42 (1989), pp. 398-412, referring to *De Opificio Mundi* 17-18 (which, he argues, reflects earlier traditions about the founding of Alexandria) and *De Providentia* 2.55 (in which the creation of the megalopolis of the cosmos in the void is compared to the founding of several cities, including Alexandria).

situation in exile, having so recently been 'governor of Alexandria, that great city (μεγαλόπολις) or multitude of cities (πολύπολις), ruler of the blest land of Egypt'.[133] In view of the fact that elsewhere Philo always uses μεγαλόπολις to describe the cosmos as a whole, it is, as Runia remarks, 'revealing that the one time Philo does call an earthly city a megalopolis, he is referring to Alexandria'.[134] Unambiguous admiration for the city of Alexandria is also expressed through the figure of the Egyptian former slave Helicon, who contemplates the honours he may receive from 'the greatest and most illustrious city of them all',[135] in exchange for promoting hostility towards the Jews of Alexandria with Gaius. We may wonder, however, to what extent such praise of the city reflects Philo's own views.

Philo expresses a more negative attitude towards the city, however, as a place unsuitable for the contemplation of higher realities, partly because of the influence of (some of) its inhabitants, but also because of his view that the wise should avoid the tumult of cities generally.[136] Accordingly, the Therapeutae, like the Essenes, avoid cities, and live away from Alexandria. The same idea governs Philo's account of the translation of the Pentateuch into Greek. Like Pseudo-Aristeas and Josephus's *Antiquities*, Philo locates the actual translating on the island of Pharos because it was quiet there.[137] Philo adds, however, that the city of Alexandria was not a suitable place for those seeking to 'make a full version of the laws given by the voice of God', because it was full of every kind of living creature and consequently disease and death, as well as the impure conduct of the healthy inhabitants.[138] The translators chose the island of Pharos for their work, not only for the sake of tranquility, but as 'the most pure place outside the city' (τὸ καθαρώτατον τῶν περὶ τὸν τόπον χωρίων ἔξω πόλεως).[139] Philo's

133. *Flacc.*, 163.
134. Runia, 'Polis and Megalopolis', p. 405.
135. *Leg. Gai.* 173.
136. *Vit. Cont.* 20; on most cities as centres of evil, particularly of impiety, see *Dec.* 2-9.
137. *Letter of Aristeas* 301, 307; Josephus, *Ant.* 12.103-104.
138. *Vit. Mos.* 2.34.
139. *Vit. Mos.* 2.34. Colson reads 'unoccupied' or, as he suggests in a note, 'the most cleanly' (p. 465), while the edition of Arnaldez *et al.* (R. Arnaldez *et al.* [eds.], *De Vita Mosis* [Paris: Cerf, 1967]) opts for 'la plus saine retraite', noting the possibility of 'l'endroit le plus dégagé' (pp. 206-207). The same word (καθαρώτατον) is used in *Vit. Mos.* 2.72 of the kind of site required for the Jewish

translators do not leave the island in the course of translating, unlike the translators in the other versions, who visit the court of Alexandria daily. Both Pseudo-Aristeas and Josephus record that the translators purified themselves on their return from the city before beginning their work, though it is not implied that this was to remove the impurity of the city.[140] Elsewhere, Philo explains that the impurity of cities, on account of their inhabitants, required that Moses receive the 'holy laws' far away from contact with such places.[141] A certain attachment to the island of Pharos, over against the city, is distinctive of Philo's version of the story: the lighthouse may be alluded to as a symbol of the Jewish Law in Philo's description of Pharos as 'the place in which the light of that version shone out'.[142] Philo stresses, finally, that, at the annual celebration of the translation on the island, both Greeks and Jews consider Pharos to be 'for the time being a more magnificent lodging than the fine mansions in the royal precincts'.[143]

Final Remarks

This discussion of Philo's attitude towards Egypt and Alexandria and their inhabitants has by no means covered every aspect of the question, but illustrates some clear points in Philo's thought. Philo

Temple, and of the place on the beach where the Jews of Alexandria make a thanksgiving prayer to God after the demise of Flaccus, which Colson renders 'the most open space' (*Flacc.* 122). In all cases, the idea of the purity of the place makes good sense as that required for the dwelling place of God or communication with God in a quasi-temple setting. In the case of our passage, the choice of a pure place for the translation of the Law is required not only because of the sacredness of the task, but also, as Philo emphasizes, to avoid the uncleanness (physical and moral) of the city of Alexandria, just as, for example, Moses, to commune with God on the mountain, had to be purified (καθαρεῦσαι) in body and soul (*Vit. Mos.* 2.68).

139.	Cf. D. Sly, *Philo's Alexandria* (London: Routledge, 1996), p. 59 who suggests that this may have been because he was 'uncomfortable' in acknowledging that many Jews had been slaves in Egypt in recent times.

140.	*Letter of Aristeas* 304-306; Josephus, *Ant.* 12.106. The *Letter of Aristeas* explains that the translators washed their hands in the sea daily as 'a token that they had done no evil' (306).

141.	*Dec.* 10-13.

142.	*Vit. Mos.* 2.41. This point is brought out by Sly, *Philo's Alexandria*, pp. 59-60.

143.	*Vit. Mos.* 2.42.

represents, more than any other Jewish writer in antiquity, an attitude of rejection and condemnation of Egyptians, making a stark differentiation between Hebrews/Jews and Egyptians. At the same time, by various means, Philo associates the Hebrews/Jews with the values of the Graeco-Roman world, constructed as antithetical to those of the Egyptians, most strikingly in the adoption of Augustan-style polemic against the Egyptians. The political function of Philo's contrasting constructions of identities is clearest in his identification of the opponents of the Alexandrian Jews as Egyptians, in order to denigrate them from a Roman perspective. Whether Philo wrote primarily as an act of self-affirmation for those of his own class within the Jewish community, or hoped to persuade a wider audience, the message is clear.

Philo's writings reveal a sense of attachment to and pride in Alexandria as his *patris*, and as the proper home of those Jews who live there. His reservations about the city as a place suitable for the contemplation of higher realities must be understood as part of his general view that cities are antipathetic to the cultivation of wisdom. Strikingly, where he does provide an unfavourable comparison with the city proper, it is to elevate the status of the island of Pharos, by virtue of its role as the birthplace of the Septuagint.

LETTERS OUT OF JUDAEA:
ECHOES OF ISRAEL IN JEWISH INSCRIPTIONS FROM EUROPE

David Noy

According to Acts 28.21, it was normal practice for the Temple authorities in pre-70 Jerusalem to exchange letters with the Jewish community in Rome, at least to warn them about suspicious people who might be visiting them:

> And they said to him [Paul], 'We have received no letters out of Judaea about you, and none of the brethren coming here has reported or spoken any evil about you'.

Several centuries later, Jews in Italy were still receiving visits from agents of the Jewish leaders in Galilee. Literature, archaeology and epigraphy provide some evidence for how much significance the land of Israel had for Jews in the European part of the Roman Empire.

Rabbinic writings show a certain amount of contact between Israel and Rome in the first and second centuries CE. In the second century, Todos (Theudas or Theodosius) of Rome was such a prestigious figure that he was permitted to encourage a practice which supposedly would have been condemned if it had been anyone else's idea: the eating of a lamb or kid in Rome at Passover.[1] The text shows rabbinic authorities claiming some power at Rome which, in this case, they declined to use; this reproduces the relationship envisaged between the Temple authorities and Rome in the first century, whether it reflects the real position in the second century or not.[2]

---

1. See *b. Beṣ.* 23a; *t. Yom Ṭob* 2, 15; *y. Pes.* 7.34a; L.V. Rutgers, *The Jews in Late Ancient Rome: Evidence of Cultural Interaction in the Roman Diaspora* (Leiden: E.J. Brill, 1995), p. 204.

2. S. Safrai, 'Relations Between the Diaspora and the Land of Israel', in S. Safrai and M. Stern (eds.), *The Jewish People in the First Century* (Assen: Van Gorcum; Philadelphia: Fortress Press, 1974), I, pp. 184-215 (210). The historical accuracy is doubted by B.M. Bokser, 'Todos and Rabbinic Authority in Rome', in J.

Leading Rabbis from the land of Israel also paid visits to Rome. Attempts made by the authorities in the first century to remove Jews from Rome were short-lived and probably of limited application, and, after the time of Claudius, there was no obstacle to Jews visiting or residing in the city. R. Aqiba, Rabban Gamaliel II, R. Eleazar b. 'Azariah and R. Joshua came there in the time of Domitian, and are described as teaching and preaching among the Roman Jews.[3] In the second century, R. Mattathiah b. Heresh settled there, establishing a *beth midrash*.[4] He was visited by R. Simeon b. Yoḥai, who had gone to Rome along with R. Eleazar b. Yose as part of a delegation. While there, R. Eleazar saw the curtain from the Holy of Holies and the High Priest's regalia.[5] In the late third or early fourth century, R. Ḥiyya b. Abba also went to Rome, as well as travelling round the eastern Diaspora.[6] There are, however, no references in the rabbinic literature to Rabbis travelling from Israel to visit other European Diaspora communities.

Other sorts of literary evidence show individual Jews moving from the East for political reasons, usually involuntarily. Josephus is the most prominent example; Berenice, Agrippa II and Herod's son Archelaus are others.[7] Some members of the Herodian family spent their youth

Neusner *et al.* (eds.), *New Perspectives on Ancient Judaism.* I. *Religion, Literature and Society in Ancient Israel: Formative Christianity and Judaism* (BJS, 206; Atlanta: Scholars Press, 1990), pp. 117-30.

3. See *b. Mak.* 24a; *m. Lam. R.* 5, 18. 1; *m. Exod. R.* 30. 9. According to *m. 'Erub.* 4.1 they sailed home from Brindisi. Cf. Safrai, 'Relations', p. 209; P. Schäfer, 'Rabbi Aqiva and Bar Kochba', in W. Scott Green (ed.), *Approaches to Ancient Judaism* (BJS, 9; Atlanta: Scholars Press, 1980), II, pp. 113-30 (114-16).

4. See *b. Sanh.* 32b; A.J. Levi, 'Gli Ebrei in Roma antica nel ricordo della Haggadà', in E. Sereni, D. Carpi, A. Milano *et al.* (eds.), *Scritti in memoria di Enzo Sereni* (Rome: Fondazione Sally Mayer, 1970), pp. 75-87; Rutgers, *The Jews*, pp. 203-204.

5. *b. Me'il.* 17 a-b; *b. Yom.* 57a; *b. Suk.* 5a; H.J. Leon, *The Jews of Ancient Rome* (Philadelphia: Jewish Publication Society of America, 1960), p. 38. The historical setting is very garbled; the delegation was sent to protest against a decree stopping sabbath-keeping and circumcision, which presumably refers to Hadrian, but the emperor's daughter is mentioned. The spoils of Jerusalem were kept in the Capitoline Temple.

6. *y. Ma'as. š.* 4. 1. 54d; *EncJud*, VII, col. 796.

7. Leon, *The Jews of Ancient Rome*, pp. 14, 31-32; H. Solin, 'Juden und Syrer im westlichen Teil der römischen Welt: Eine ethnisch-demographische Studie mit besonderer Berücksichtigung der sprachlichen Zustände', *ANRW*, II.29.2,

in Rome before returning to Judaea. A man claiming to be Herod's son Alexander won support among Jews at Puteoli and Rome, indicating a continued interest in events in Judaea among the Jews who had settled in Italy—the real Alexander had earlier lived at Rome in the house of Asinius Pollio.[8]

Archaeology has provided further evidence. Trade clearly took place between Judaea and the West. The evidence for it is from the first century CE: amphorae labelled Ἰουδαϊκός from Pompeii, and an amphora from Ibiza with Hebrew lettering similar to some found at Masada.[9] The existence of local Jewish populations may have created the demand for Judaean produce; the trade that resulted could have been another motive for some Jews to settle in the West. Part of the Vigna Randanini catacomb at Rome, probably no earlier than the late second century CE, contains a number of *kokhim*. These are burial places cut into the gallery wall at ground level, so that the body could lie at right angles to the gallery (whereas in a normal *loculus* it lay parallel), with a ledge to enable two bodies to be placed in one *kokh*. This type of grave is almost unparalleled in Europe, but was common in the eastern Mediterranean area, and especially in the land of Israel. Rutgers notes that the Vigna Randanini *kokhim* are very similar to those of the 'Tomb of the Prophets' on the Mount of Olives.[10] It is likely that this style of tomb was brought to Rome from Israel, either by immigrants or at least by people who had visited the Jerusalem area.

Some Jews, perhaps the majority of immigrants up to 135 CE, came to the West through being enslaved. Philo attributes the origin of the Jewish community of Rome to prisoners who were brought to Italy and then emancipated.[11] These would presumably have been captured by Pompey in 63 BCE, although in fact there must have been a Jewish community in Rome earlier than that.[12] Smaller numbers of slaves may have resulted from smaller-scale wars such as those of Cassius in 37 BCE and Varus in 4 BCE, disturbances like the anti-census protests

pp. 590-789, 1222-49 (659-661); C. Vismara, 'I cimiteri ebraici di Roma', in A. Giardina (ed.), *Società romana e impero tardoantico* II (Bari: Laterza, 1986), pp. 351-503 (351-55).

8.   Josephus, *War.* 2.101-10; *Ant.* 15.342-43, 17.324-38.

9.   *JIWE* I.40, 178.

10.   Rutgers, *The Jews*, pp. 61-65.

11.   Philo, *Leg. Gai.* 155.

12.   Leon, *The Jews of Ancient Rome*, p. 5.

of 6 CE, and Herod's policy of selling brigands into slavery.[13] Further waves of prisoners would have arrived after the revolts of the first and early second centuries CE. Enormous numbers of prisoners were captured during 66–70 CE: for example, after the fall of Tarichaeae in 67, 6,000 prisoners were sent to work on the Corinthian Canal and another 30,400 were sold as slaves.[14] Even if only a small proportion were eventually sent westwards, the numbers involved must have been considerable. In the eighth century and later, Jews in Southern Italy claimed descent from Titus's captives,[15] and although Titus himself would hardly have settled them in cities like Oria, the genealogical claim is in itself plausible.

Philo takes an optimistic view of the chances of Jewish slaves at Rome obtaining freedom through the help of fellow Jews. Existing Jewish communities in the Diaspora were encouraged to 'ransom' (i.e. buy and manumit) Jewish slaves with whom they came into contact, although this must have been difficult when newly arrived slaves were so numerous. Many Jewish slaves must in fact have ended their lives in slavery, and these are the least likely to have left any record. However, one epitaph from Naples shows what happened to a woman who was captured during the revolt of 66–70:

> Claudia Aster, prisoner from Jerusalem. Tiberius Claudius [Pro]culus, imperial freedman, took care (of the epitaph). I ask you to make sure you take care that no-one casts down my inscription contrary to the law. She lived twenty-five years.[16]

Although enslaved, she was freed before her death. The man who commemorated her, a freedman of Claudius or Nero, may also have been her owner/patron, and/or her husband. An epitaph from Athens records 'Ammia of Jerusalem', who may have been another victim of the revolt, but there is no further information in her case.[17] Aster probably owed her manumission to one man rather than to the whole local community, and there is a parallel story in rabbinic sources. The

13. A. Kasher, 'The Nature of Jewish Migration in the Mediterranean Countries in the Hellenistic-Roman Era', *Mediterranean History Review* 2 (1987), pp. 46-75 (50-51); Rutgers, *The Jews*, p. 168.

14. Josephus, *War* 3.540.

15. The claim is made both in appendices to the *Book of Josippon* and in the *Chronicle of Aḥimaaz*, cf. Kasher, 'The Nature', p. 53.

16. *JIWE* I.26.

17. *CII* I².715a.

future R. Ishmael b. Elisha was also captured at Jerusalem in 70 CE as a child, and was later ransomed from slavery at Rome by R. Joshua b. Hananiah, who apparently found him working as a prostitute.[18]

Epitaphs and literary passages that complement each other are very unusual. Epitaphs alone are the source of information for the lives of most European Jews. This form of evidence is somewhat distorted, because by far the largest part comes from the city of Rome, and nearly all comes from the third century CE or later. Most of the epitaphs follow restricted patterns that leave little room for self-expression. Thus only a few are informative enough to show that someone had, for example, come as an immigrant from the land of Israel or had dealings with someone sent from Israel. They do not normally show why the immigration occurred.

An epitaph from Rome commemorates an immigrant from Tiberias:

> Alypius of Tiberias and his sons Justus and Alypius, Hebrews, with their father rest here.[19]

There are rabbinic references to an Alypius who gave financial help to R. Simeon b. Abba of Tiberias in the third century, and it is possible that the same man went to Rome, but Alypius was not an unusual name.[20] Other Tiberians are commemmorated at Salona (Aurelius Dionysius) and in Laconia (Justus son of Andromache).[21] 'Ionius, also called Akone, of Sepphoris' was buried in the Monteverde catacomb at Rome.[22] It has been suggested that he is to be identified with Bar Yohannis of Sepphoris, who is mentioned in a rabbinic text.[23]

Caesarea was the place of origin of another man buried at Monteverde:

18. *b. Giṭ.* 58a; *m. Lam. R.* 4.2.4; *EncJud* IX, col. 84. There is an even more improbable story of R. Zadok II also being enslaved, and his female owner manumitting him when she found out about his priestly status, cf. *EncJud* XVI, col. 915.

19. *JIWE* II.561.

20. *y. Bikk.* 3.3.65d; *y. B. Meṣ* 2.3.8c.

21. *CII* I².680, 721a.

22. *JIWE* II.60.

23. S. Klein, 'Bar-Yohannis of Sepphoris at Rome', *BJPES* 7 (1940), pp. 47-51 (Hebrew with English summary), citing *m. Est. R.* 39-40, 2.4 (I owe this reference to Susan Weingarten). Bar-Yohannis gave a banquet for the 'notables of Rome', but this probably refers to Roman provincial officers rather than people in the city of Rome.

Here lies Macedonius the Hebrew from Caesarea in Palestine, son of Alexander. The memory of the righteous one for a blessing. In peace your sleep.[24]

The second sentence quotes Prov. 10.7 using the version of Aquila. The final sentence is the commonest formula of the Jewish epitaphs from Rome, showing that Macedonius, or, at least, his commemorator, had been well assimilated to local epigraphic customs. Other epitaphs recording Jews from Caesarea are also likely to refer to the Palestinian city, although they could mean one of the other Caesareas.[25]

There is very little evidence for migration in the other direction. At Jerusalem there are epitaphs for Maria wife of Alexander from Capua and for the proselyte Miriam of Delos; perhaps also Judah from Laconia.[26] No other burials in the land of Israel are explicitly said to contain Jews of European origin; there are none at Beth She'arim.

Aristobulus II was poisoned at Rome in 49 BCE and his remains were taken back to Judaea to the Hasmonaean tomb,[27] but he was only a temporary exile. It is possible anyway that European Jews could be buried in Israel without ever having lived there; burial or reburial there was encouraged by the Rabbis at least from the third century CE.[28] It was also possible to die while on pilgrimage. Visits to the Temple for the main festivals would have been made by those who could afford them until 70, but pilgrim visits to the land of Israel presumably ended after that.[29]

Individuals in epitaphs are occasionally labelled 'Hebrew' ('Εβραῖος/ *hebraeus*), like Macedonius, or 'Jew' ('Ιουδαῖος/*Iudaeus*).[30] 'Hebrew' is used for individuals at Naples and Rome;[31] all but one of the people

24. *JIWE* II.112.
25. *JIWE* I.30 (Naples); II.459 (Villa Torlonia at Rome); *CII* I.715 (Athens).
26. *CII* II.1284 (written on an ossuary, so probably not later than first century CE), 1390; Safrai, 'Relations', p. 194.
27. Josephus, *War* 1.184; *Ant.* 14.124.
28. I. Gafni, 'Reinterment in the Land of Israel: Notes on the Origin and Development of the Custom', *Jerusalem Cathedra* 1 (1981), pp. 96-104.
29. Acts 2.9-11 lists 'visitors from Rome' among the Diaspora Jews present at Rome for Pentecost, cf. Safrai, 'Relations', pp. 193-94.
30. According to Tertullian, *Apol.* 18.6, 'they were formerly *Hebraei* who are now *Iudaei*', but this does not fit the chronology of the inscriptions (or of general usage in Latin literature). The terms seem to be interchangeable in, for example, the letters of Gregory the Great, cf. Solin, 'Juden und Syrer', p. 650.
31. Naples: *JIWE* I.33 (a man named Numerius), 35 (Crescentia), 37 (Flaes, ? =

thus designated are male. 'Jew' is slightly rarer for individuals at Rome, but commoner elsewhere in western Europe; it can apply to a proselyte as well as to a born Jew, and is common for both genders.[32] In a Jewish catacomb, there was no reason to note simply that the deceased was Jewish, so the use of either of these terms in a clearly Jewish context appears to have some further significance.

There was a synagogue of the Hebrews at Rome.[33] Thus it seems that in inscriptions 'Hebrew' cannot simply be an alternative to 'Jew'. La Piana and Leon suggested that the first synagogue at Rome was called the 'synagogue of the Hebrews', so that only later ones had to have more imaginative names.[34] However, a Jewish community, probably that of Ostia, is described as *Iudeorum* in an inscription from Castel Porziano, and at Reggio di Calabria what appears to be a building inscription from the synagogue ends τῶν Ἰουδαίων.[35] At Panticapaeum in the Crimea, the synagogue (in the sense of community) was τῶν Ἰουδαίων, and at Intercisa in Pannonia it was *Iudeorum*.[36] Thus, it would have been more natural to call the first Roman synagogue 'synagogue of the Jews', although admittedly the term 'synagogue of the Hebrews' seems to have been used at Corinth (a very fragmentary inscription) and at Philadelphia in Lydia.[37]

It has also been suggested, mainly on the basis of the contrast of

---

Flavius). Rome: *JIWE* II.44 (Julianus), 108 (Monimus also called Eusabbatis), 112 (Macedonius), 559 (Caelius Quintus), 561 (Alypius, Justus and Alypius).

32. Rome: *JIWE* II.183 (a woman from Laodicea), 233, 489 (see below, pp. 113-14), 491 (a proselyte), 567 (reading uncertain). Western Europe: *JIWE* I.7, 8, 179, 188 (all epitaphs from apparently non-Jewish contexts). Eastern Europe: *CII* I.678, 680, 697, 701 (?), 709, 710, *CII* I^2.690b, 711b, 715i. Solin, 'Juden und Syrer', pp. 647-49; R.S. Kraemer, 'On the Meaning of the Term "Jew" in Greco-Roman Inscriptions', *HTR* 82 (1989), pp. 35-53.

33. This is made explicit in *JIWE* II.578-79, which record the family of the 'father of the synagogue'. *JIWE* II.2 and 33 refer respectively to an *exarchon* and an *archon* of the Hebrews, without using the term 'synagogue'.

34. G. la Piana, 'Foreign Groups in Rome during the First Centuries of the Empire', *HTR* 20 (1927), pp. 183-403 (356); Leon, *The Jews of Ancient Rome*, pp. 148-49, also summarizing earlier suggestions; M. Stern, 'The Jewish Diaspora', in Safrai and Stern (eds.), *The Jewish People in the First Century*, I, pp. 117-83 (167); P.W. van der Horst, *Ancient Jewish Epitaphs* (Kampen: Kok, 1991), pp. 87-88.

35. *JIWE* I.18; 139.

36. *CII* I.683; 684; *CII* I^2.683b, 677. Probably also on Samos: *CII* I^2.731f.

37. *CII* I.718; II.754.

'Hebrews' with 'Hellenists' in Acts 6.1, that people designated as *Hebraios* were speakers of Hebrew or Aramaic.[38] However, none of the Roman inscriptions for individual 'Hebrews' uses any Hebrew or Aramaic; three from Naples all end with a *shalom* formula, but so do the other epitaphs from the same group which do not commemorate a 'Hebrew'.[39] Only one of the four inscriptions mentioning officers of the synagogue of the Hebrews uses any Hebrew or Aramaic.[40] Another view that has been proposed by, among others, Frey, and recently supported by van der Horst and van Henten, is that the 'Hebrews' are Jews who came from, or had especially close ties with, the land of Israel.[41] This fits the epitaphs of Macedonius and Alypius, although none of the other people said to originate from Israel is described as 'Hebrew', and most 'Hebrews' have Latin names.[42]

The term 'Israelite' occurs once, in a puzzling inscription commemorating a three-year-old girl who seems to be described as Εἰουδέα Ἰσδραηλίτης.[43] It is also Paul's designation of himself in Romans 11.1, whereas in Phil. 3.5 he calls himself Ἐβραῖος ἐξ Ἐβραίων.[44] In 2 Cor. 11.22 the two designations are alternatives:

---

38. See, for example, K.G. Kuhn and W. Gutbrod in *TDNT*, III, pp. 367-69, 372-75. Both make alternative suggestions. Kuhn proposes that *Hebraios* avoided contemptuous overtones which *Ioudaios* acquired; Gutbrod that it denotes someone of 'Palestinian nationality' (see further below), if not necessarily a speaker of Aramaic. Leon (*The Jews of Ancient Rome*, p. 148) gives references to other proponents of the language explanation.

39. *JIWE* I.31-35.

40. *JIWE* II.33.

41. Frey (*CII* I, pp. lxxvi-lxxvii); J.Z. Smith, 'Fences and Neighbors: Some Contours of Early Judaism', in Green (ed.), *Approaches*, II, pp. 1-26 (19); Solin, 'Juden und Syrer', p. 649; van der Horst, *Ancient Jewish Epitaphs*, p. 70; J.W. van Henten, 'A Jewish Epitaph in a Literary Text: 4 Macc. 17.8-10', in J.W. van Henten and P.W. van der Horst (eds.), *Studies in Early Jewish Epigraphy* (Leiden: E.J. Brill, 1994), pp. 44-69 (52); *JIWE* II.44.

42. See n. 31. Solin ('Juden und Syrer', p. 648), dismisses the possibility that *Ioudaios* indicates someone connected with Judaea, partly on the grounds of the numerous *Ioudaioi* with Latin names.

43. *JIWE* II.489. Lines 1-4 read: Εἰρήνη τρεζπτὴ προσήλυτος πατρὸς καὶ μητρὸς Εἰουδέα Ἰσδραηλίτης. It is very unclear which epithets refer to the parents and which to Irene herself. τρεζπτὴ is usually taken as a form of θρεπτή.

44. R. Murray, 'Jews, Hebrews and Christians: Some Needed Distinctions', *NovT* 24.3 (1982), pp. 194-208 (204) suggests that the latter passage refers to the language.

Are they Hebrews? So am I. Are they Israelites? So am I.

'Israelite' in the inscription seems somehow to reinforce 'Jew', but it is not clear how. The girl also seems from the wording of the inscription to be a proselyte (perhaps adopted into a Jewish family, or part of a family who all converted) so there is probably no connection with geographic origin.[45]

A further source of contact between Europe and the land of Israel was the practice of sending money eastwards. While the Temple stood, Diaspora Jews living in the Roman Empire were able to send their annual contributions with the state's approval; Josephus shows that money was being sent from Rome in the first century CE.[46] After 70 the money was diverted to the state instead, but there is evidence that, at least by the fourth century, the Patriarch (*Nasi*) was undertaking fund-raising in the West: the legal text that abolishes the right of the Patriarch to send out *apostoli* to collect money is addressed to the Praetorian Prefect of Italy and Africa.[47]

There are other legal texts mentioning 'patriarchs' among Jewish leaders, but they do not make it clear if they are referring to local officers, or to the Patriarch in Tiberias.[48] There are no inscriptions clearly referring to individual local patriarchs, so when an unnamed 'patriarch' occurs in an inscription it seems most likely that it means the one in Tiberias. In an inscription from the synagogue at Stobi in Macedonia, dated probably to 281 CE,[49] an enormous fine was payable to the Patriarch by anyone who violated the arrangements for the building made by Ti. Claudius Polycharmus. In this case only Jews needed to know who the Patriarch was; they would be the only ones

45. The term 'Israelites' is also used for Samaritans in an inscription from Delos (Ph. Brunneau, *BCH* 106 [1982], pp. 465-504), but hardly seems likely to have that sense here.

46. Josephus, *Ant.* 18.81-84. In general, on payment of the Temple tax in the Diaspora, see Safrai, 'Relations', pp. 188-91.

47. *C. Theo.* 16.8.14 (399).

48. *C. Theo.* 16.8.1 (315); 16.8.2 (330); 16.8.13 (397). See F. Millar, 'The Jews of the Graeco-Roman Diaspora between Paganism and Christianity, AD 312-438', in J. Lieu, J. North and T. Rajak (eds.), *The Jews among Pagans and Christians in the Roman Empire* (London: Routledge, 1992), pp. 97-123 (98).

49. *CII* I and *CII* I².694; L. Levine, *The Rabbinic Class of Roman Palestine in Late Antiquity* (Jerusalem; New York: Yad Izhak Ben-Zvi, English edn, 1989), p. 138.

affected by the proviso.[50] The implication is that the Patriarch had enough influence in Macedonia to be able to collect the fine.

In a third- or fourth-century Greek inscription from Argos,[51] Aurelius Joses, calling on various forms of protection for his tomb, invoked, among other things, 'the honour of the patriarchs and the honour of the ethnarchs'. At Catania in 383, Aurelius Samohil invoked in Latin 'the honours of the patriarchs' for the same purpose.[52] The latter inscription, at least, comes from a time when the Patriarch was a particularly prestigious figure in the Empire. The threats are meant to be sufficient to deter grave-violators, which ought to mean non-Jews as well as Jews, so they have to use deterrents whose power can be felt outside Jewish circles; thus it is much more likely that the inscriptions mean the Patriarchs in Tiberias rather than the biblical patriarchs. In the Argos inscription, 'patriarchs' may refer to Abraham, Isaac and Jacob, and 'ethnarchs' to the Jewish leaders in Tiberias (for whom Origen also seems to use the designation 'ethnarch').[53]

Fund-raising continued after the patriarchate was abolished in the 420s. In 429, money collected from Diaspora synagogues by Jewish leaders, a practice existing 'since the demise of the Patriarchs', was ordered to be confiscated to the treasury.[54] An epitaph from Venosa which is probably from the early sixth century[55] states that 'two apostles and two Rabbis' spoke the dirges for the deceased girl. Since the date is too late for these to be the Patriarch's emissaries, the apostles are probably people sent from Israel according to the practice objected to in 429—Byzantine law would not have applied in Venosa at this date. In early ninth-century Venosa there was 'a man who had come from the Land of Israel, profoundly learned in the law of God, a master of wisdom', perhaps another in the same tradition.[56]

Individuals designated as Rabbi (*rebbi* in Latin) may also have had some direct or indirect connection with Israel, if their title was acquired

---

50. The earlier dating previously accepted would make it less likely that the Patriarch himself rather than a local official is meant, see Millar, 'The Jews of the Graeco-Roman Diaspora', p. 100.

51. *CII* I.719.

52. *JIWE* I.145.

53. Origen, *Ep. ad Africanum* 14.

54. *C. Theo.* 16.8.29.

55. *JIWE* I.86.

56. *Chronicle of Ahimaaz* 4b.

through what became the standard ordination process. They occur in two fourth- to sixth-century inscriptions from Campania.[57] However, Cohen suggests that such Rabbis might be locally ordained and did not necessarily have any link with the 'rabbinic' authorities in Israel.[58]

People who had no connection with the land of Israel themselves could still have some reference to it when they were commemorated. There are indirect references to the Temple in the symbols used on many of the inscriptions, especially the menorah (which is never shown in the form with an octagonal base depicted on the Arch of Titus at Rome). However, people using this were not necessarily thinking of the Temple itself, but only of the symbols of Judaism. One gold-glass has a representation of the Temple, apparently at the Feast of Tabernacles, with a menorah in the pediment and *sukkoth* outside; there is a Greek inscription referring to the 'house of peace'.[59] The gold-glass is probably third or early fourth century, but was actually found in a Christian catacomb (SS Pietro and Marcellino, Via Casilina). The presence at Rome of the spoils of Jerusalem, and the very prominent commemoration of the destruction of the Temple on the Arch of Titus, may have served as regular reminders of Jerusalem to the Jews of Rome, but do not appear to have had a direct effect on their art.

Some epitaphs refer explicitly to 'Israel'. It can be an individual word in Hebrew characters,[60] or part of the fairly frequent formula, שלום על ישראל, 'peace upon Israel', which could be added to an otherwise Greek or Latin inscription.[61] There are references in Latin epitaphs to *Deus Israel* and to sleep *cum omne Israel*.[62] In all these cases, Israel almost certainly signifies the whole Jewish nation rather than the geographical land of Israel. In the long metrical inscription from the Monteverde catacomb at Rome, which commemorates a woman called Regina, she is described as someone 'who deserved to have an abode in the venerable country'[63]. The land referred to (using

---

57. *JIWE* I.22, 36. Also in early mediaeval inscriptions, e.g. an eighth-or ninth-century inscription from Mérida in Spain, see *JIWE* I.197.

58. S.J.D. Cohen, 'Epigraphical Rabbis', *JQR* 72 (1981–1982), pp. 1-17.

59. *JIWE* II.588, with bibliography.

60. *JIWE* II.186.

61. Rome: *JIWE* II.193, 529. Venosa: *JIWE* I.61. Sicily: *JIWE* I.145. Sardinia: *JIWE* I.173. Spain: *JIWE* I.183; 185. Gaul: *JIWE* I.189.

62. *JIWE* I.174,187.

63. *JIWE* I.103 (with bibliography): *quae meruit sedem venerandi ruris habere.*

the Latin *rus*) is probably the Garden of Eden (Frey) or Paradise (Cumont), but there is a possibility that Regina's resurrection is envisaged as taking place in the land of Israel (Fischer, Maser, Delling); van der Horst leaves the question open. There is no other evidence for Jews in Europe expecting resurrection at all, in their actual burial places or in Israel.

One other piece of information shows that the land of Israel was a focus for the thoughts of European Jews. In the synagogue at Ostia, the fourth-century adaptations which gave it its final form included the installation of a permanent torah-shrine, which would have been the centre of attention during services: a semi-circular *opus vittatum* wall at the top of four steps, fronted by two Corinthian columns on which rested architraves with Jewish symbols carved in low relief.[64] The existing layout of the main hall would have made it natural to place the shrine on the wall facing the entrance. Instead, it was built into the same wall as the entrance, so that someone coming into the hall had to turn 180° in order to face it. It was orientated to point to the south-east, so that those facing it during worship were also facing Jerusalem.

64. *JIWE* II.13, with full bibliography.

THE PATRIOTIC RABBI:
BABYLONIAN SCHOLARS IN ROMAN PERIOD PALESTINE

Joshua Schwartz

Introduction

Patriotism is not a phrase often associated with Rabbis of the ancient world in general or with those living during Roman rule in Palestine or Persian rule in Babylonia.[1] There might have been an occasional Rabbi who had a kind thought to say about Roman rule in Palestine or Sasanian rule in Babylonia, and some of the Rabbis may have even had political ties with the Romans or Persians, but they were hardly distinguished by such sentiments or ties and it is not this type of patriotism that I wish to discuss.[2] Nor am I interested in whether

1.   Needless to say, rabbinic chronology is different from general chronology of the ancient world. Although Roman rule in Palestine encompasses both the period of the Mishnah, or the Tannaitic period (approximately 70–220 CE), and the period of the Talmud, or the Amoraic period (approximately 220–450 CE), the majority of traditions relevant for this discussion date from the period of approximately 200–400 CE and most of my comments, therefore, will pertain to this time. The lack of either earlier or later traditions reflects, for the most part, the vagaries of Talmudic literature and the problematic nature of this literature for the study of history and not necessarily changes or developments in the trends I shall study. I shall, therefore, make use of the occasional tradition outside of the basic time framework I have just established. My few references to Babylonia will refer to the period of Sasanian rule which began with the reign of Ardashir I (226-241 CE). On the history of this period in general see J. Neusner, *A History of the Jews in Babylonia*, I–V (SPB, 9; Leiden: E.J. Brill, 1965–1970).

2.   The attitudes of the Rabbis and Sages to the sovereign powers of the ancient world is beyond the purview of this discussion. It is not surprising that often their views were quite negative, but this was not always the case. See, for example, I. Ben-Shalom, 'Rabbi Judah B. Ilai's Attitude Towards Rome', *Zion* 49 (1984), pp. 9-24 (Hebrew); D. Rokeah, 'On "R. Judah B. Ilai's Attitude Toward Rome"', *Zion* 52 (1987), pp. 107-10 (Hebrew) and I. Ben-Shalom, 'On R. Judah B. Ilai's Attitude Towards Rome: A Rejoinder', *Zion* 52 (1987), pp. 111-13 (Hebrew).

Babylonian Sages in Palestine transferred their allegiance to the Roman Empire or whether they remained at heart Sasanian patriots in spite of the hostile environment of a Roman province.

I am also not concerned with the local patriotism of the Rabbis in either Palestine or Babylonia. Thus, there may have been Rabbis, along with other city residents, both Jewish and non-Jewish, who took pride in the buildings, institutions and status of their cities, whether in Palestine or Babylonia,[3] but this is not the patriotism with which I shall be concerned. Rather, I shall discuss local Torah patriotism.

Before I begin, however, it is necessary to explain briefly the historical background of the period. Thus, during a good part of the period of Roman rule in Palestine, there was a large immigration of Babylonian Jews to Palestine.[4] Much of this immigration was composed of Rabbis, particularly young ones, who were often bachelors, although a number did have families, some brought along and some left behind in Babylonia.[5] Also, many of the Rabbis could best be described more as students than as Sages, although all belonged to what may be called the rabbinic class or the elite.[6]

It is my intention to try and portray the perceptions of these Babylonian Rabbis or students regarding their new status upon arriving in Palestine. What did they feel regarding the Torah world of their new country, its academies, institutions and Rabbis? Did they themselves become 'Palestinian' Rabbis, not just in the technical geographic sense, but in terms of identifying with Palestinian Torah and institutions; or

3. On local patriotism in Roman Palestine see J. Geiger, 'Local Patriotism in Hellenistic Cities in Palestine', in A. Kasher, G. Fuks and U. Rappaport (eds.), *Greece and Rome in Eretz-Israel: Collected Essays* (Jerusalem: Yad Izhak Ben-Zvi, Israel Exploration Society, 1989), pp. 261-69 (Hebrew). On aspects of local patriotism in Jewish cities in Palestine see, for example, S. Miller, 'Intercity Relations in Roman Palestine: The Case of Sepphoris and Tiberias', *Association for Jewish Studies Review* 12 (1987), pp. 1-24. On Babylonia see I. Gafni, 'Expressions and Types of "Local Patriotism" among the Jews of Sasanian Babylonia', in S. Shaked and A. Netzer (eds.), *Irano-Judaica* (Jerusalem: Ben-Zvi Institute, 1990), II, pp. 63-71.

4. See J. Schwartz, 'Aliyah from Babylonia During the Amoraic Period (200-500 CE)', *The Jerusalem Cathedra* 3 (1983), pp. 58-69 and the bibliography cited there.

5. Schwartz, 'Aliyah from Babylonia'. Cf. J. Schwartz, 'Babylonian Commoners in Amoraic Palestine', *JAOS* 101 (1981), pp. 317-22.

6. See in general L.I. Levine, *The Rabbinic Class of Roman Palestine in Late Antiquity* (Jerusalem: Yad Izhak Ben-Zvi, 1989).

was their new affiliation only surface-deep, and, in spite of their best intentions, did they ultimately remain Babylonians in spirit and at heart, even if perhaps they were not always aware of it? Also, I shall try and determine what they felt about their native land and its Rabbis? Did they leave Babylonia because of negative feelings regarding Babylonia, or was it the positive feelings regarding Palestine which drew them to that country and its rabbinic institutions? Or, perhaps, was it a combination of both factors which brought them to Palestine? In addition to all this, it is likely that their attitudes and perceptions were also shaped by the comments and views of those who remained behind in Babylonia. Therefore, we shall also examine some views of the Babylonian Sages who elected to stay at home.

It is also important to determine how and indeed whether the perceptions of the Babylonians were related to their reception in Palestine. Were they 'insiders', or 'outsiders'? In other words, it is not just a question of whether the Babylonians wanted to become Palestinian Rabbis, but also of whether the local rabbinic aristocracy was willing to let them in and what was expected of those Babylonians who were let in.[7]

Perceptions and Attitudes: Talmudic Tradition

The clearest exposition of a Babylonian Sage regarding the reasons for his leaving Babylonia and moving to Palestine are found in the words of the third century CE Sage, R. Eleazar b. Pedat, in *y. Roš Haš.* 2. 58b:

> And R. Leazar [Eleazar] said: 'And my hand shall be against the prophets that see vanity, and that divine lies' (Ezek. 13.9). [The continuation of the verse states] 'they shall not be in the council [lit. *sod* (secret)] of My peo-

7. A complete exposition of all these points would take us far beyond the space allotted for this study and the discussion, therefore, will for the most part attempt to point out the general trends involved in the perceptions and reactions mentioned above. Also, the use of Talmudic material, basically the only material at our disposal, is not without its problems, specifically as to whether individual sources can be used at times to describe general trends or developments or whether literary motifs in some of these traditions may outweigh the historical or sociological content or value of the traditions. However, even literary motifs may contribute to historical understanding. See, for example, R. Kalmin, 'Rabbinic Attitudes Toward Rabbis as a Key to the Dating of Talmudic Sources', *JQR* 84 (1993), pp. 1-28. In any case, I shall refrain from discussing methodological issues of Talmudics unless absolutely necessary.

ple'—this is the secret of the intercalation of the calendar. 'Neither shall they be written in the register of the house of Israel'—this is appointment. 'Neither shall they enter into the land of Israel'—this is the Land of Israel. And R. Leazar said: When I came here [to the Land of Israel], the first [curse] was removed. When I was appointed, the second [curse] was removed. When I went up to intercalate the year, the third was removed.

R. Eleazar's comments regarding his home country are devastating. Babylonia in his view was a spiritual and intellectual wasteland. The 'false prophets' there, the Babylonian Sages and Rabbis (!), will never attain the spiritual and intellectual rights and privileges that Rabbis and Sages could receive in Palestine, such as full rabbinic ordination, the right to participate in the intercalation of the calendar and the very atmosphere of the land of Israel.[8] True, there will be future Divine retribution against the 'false prophets', but for the moment the curses could be removed only by leaving Babylonia and going to Palestine. Only a Palestinian Sage, Rabbi or scholar could fulfil his scholarly potential through the numerous rights and privileges available to Rabbis in Palestine, but not to those in Babylonia. The only other option available to those Babylonian Rabbis was to remain in Babylonia and to endure the curses of the 'false prophets' of that rabbinic society.

R. Eleazar, therefore, mentions two factors. On the one hand, there was an extremely negative view of Babylonia, while, on the other hand, Palestine was the land of rabbinic opportunity. However, leaving one country and going to another was not sufficient to remove the 'taint of Babylonia'; success in Palestinian rabbinic society was imperative.

Before I go on to discuss further the attitudes of the Babylonian Rabbis in Palestine and their reception in that country, I should point out that Babylonian rabbinic society had not exactly been ungenerous to these young Babylonian Rabbis and scholars and most had already been recognized as outstanding scholars in the Babylonian academies of Pumpeditha and Sura.[9] Consequently, the Babylonian masters who chose to stay in their homeland clearly could not ignore the dangers inherent in the violent anti-Babylonian sentiment of some of their best

8. On these concepts see Schwartz, 'Aliyah from Babylonia', p. 59.
9. R. Hananiah (*b. B. Meṣ.* 6b), R. Assi (*y. 'Erub.* 5.22d; *y. Ter.* 1. 40a), R. Zeira (*b. Qid.* 39a; *b. Šab.* 41a), R. Abba (*b. Ber.* 11b, 24b) and R. Hoshaiah II (*b. Giṭ.* 25a; *b. B. Meṣ* 43b), for instance, had been associated with Pumpeditha, while R. Zeira (*b. Ber.* 39a; *b. Men.* 39a), R. Abba (*b. B. Qam.* 102a; *b. Naz.* 13a) and R. Hoshaiah II (*b. Ber.* 37b), for instance, had also been associated with Sura.

students since, after all, such sentiments left unchecked might empty
out their academies. These Rabbis tried to fight the 'curses' mentioned
above with a similar type of ammunition. Thus, Rav Judah bar Ezekiel,
the head of the Babylonian academy at Pumpiditha stated in *b. Ket.*
110b-111a that:

> All who go up from Babylonia to the Land of Israel transgress against a
> positive commandment as it is written, 'They shall be carried to Babylon,
> and there shall they remain until the day that I remember them, saith the
> Lord' (Jeremiah 27.22).

The success, however, of such sentiments was apparently limited and
Rav Judah was not even able to prevent a number of his own students
from leaving Babylonia without seeking his permission, something
rarely done in a master–disciple relationship.[10]

The Babylonian masters had good reasons for trying to prevent
their young colleagues and students from leaving Babylonia. Many of
these young Babylonian immigrant Rabbis were apparently quite
successful in cleansing themselves of the curse of Babylonia and succeeding in their intellectual and spiritual quests in Palestine. To cite
just a few of the success stories of these Babylonians in Palestine:
Hillel the Elder became the head of the Sanhedrin in Jerusalem at the
end of the Second Temple period (*y. Pes.* 6. 33a); R. Nathan, the son
of the Babylonian Exilarch, was appointed *Av Beth Din* in the court
and academy of the late second century CE patriarch, Rabban Simeon
b. Gamaliel (*b. Hor.* 13b); R. Hanina b. Hama was head of the academy at Sepphoris (*y. Šab.* 16, 6c); R. Eleazar and R. Ammi were the
heads of the academy at Tiberias;[11] the Babylonians R. Ammi and R.
Assi were called the 'judges of the Land of Israel' (*b. Sanh.* 17b) and
their Babylonian colleagues, R. Hoshaiah and R. Haninah, were
referred to as 'the holy Rabbis in the Land of Israel' (*b. Pes.* 113b).
This is not to say that every Babylonian who came to Palestine broke
into the scholarly and intellectual hierarchy of Palestinian rabbinic
circles, but the extent of their success went far beyond anything that
might have been expected based on their numbers in this society.[12]

10. Both R. Zeira (*b. Šab.* 41a) and R. Abba, for instance, (*b. Ber.* 24b) left
without seeking the permission of Rav Judah or even taking some type of formal
leave.

11. See B.M Levin (ed.), *Iggeret Rav Sherira Gaon* (Haifa: Godah-Itsqovski,
1921), p. 84.

12. We know the names of almost ninety Babylonian Rabbis who emigrated to

R. Eleazar, therefore, seemed to be correct in his description of the aspirations of his fellow rabbinic immigrants. There were apparently, however, somewhat different points of view among his Babylonian immigrant colleagues regarding their homeland. *b. Pes.* 87b provides three different views:

> R. Hiyya taught: What is meant by the verse, 'God understandeth the way thereof, and He knoweth the place thereof' (Job 28.23)? The Holy One Blessed be He knoweth that Israel are unable to endure cruel decrees of Edom [Rome], therefore he exiled them to Babylonia.

The third century CE former Babylonian sage R. Hiyya was rich and from the family of the exilarch.[13] He was not burning any bridges. Palestine was Palestine, but Babylonia also played an important role in Jewish history since, in his view at least, the favorable conditions there facilitated the continued existence of the Jewish people.[14] The tradition continues:

> R. Eleazar (b. Pedat) also said—The Holy One Blessed be He exiled Israel to Babylonia only because it is as deep as *she'ol*.

R. Eleazar appears to be consistent regarding his view of Babylonia. There was nothing positive about life there; it was a punishment and 'buried' any attempts at a fruitful Jewish life.

The third view, that of the former Babylonian sage, R. Hanina b. Hama, who, as stated above, became the head of the academy in Sepphoris, appears to be something of a compromise: 'R. Hanina said: Because their language is akin to the language of Torah'. Babylonia is exile, but at least it does allow for Jewish existence.

Palestine during the Roman period. Bearing in mind the fact that Talmudic literature usually mentions only the most prominent Rabbis, there were, therefore, numerous junior immigrant scholars and Rabbis not cited by name, or mentioned at all, who moved from Babylonia to Palestine. Some of these Rabbis may have exaggerated their own capabilities, or have had exaggerated expectations regarding their absorption into the upper echelons of the Palestinian rabbinic elite and, therefore, were not successful. Cf. J. Schwartz, 'Tension Between Palestinian Scholars and Babylonian Olim in Amoraic Palestine', *JSJ* 11 (1980), pp. 78-94.

13. See A. Hyman, *Sefer Toldot Tannaim we-Amoraim* (London: Express, 1910), I, pp. 424-34.

14. It is quite possible, though, that the view of R. Hiyya here is just pro-Babylonian propaganda inserted in the name of R. Hiyya. This would not be so unusual in the Baylonian Talmud. See, for example, I. Gafni, 'The Babylonian *Yeshiva* as Reflected in Bava Qamma 117a', *Tarbiz* 49 (1979), pp. 292-301.

Thus, the views of at least some of the former Babylonians regarding the Jewish community of their native country were somewhat positive. It should be pointed out, though, that these positive comments applied to Jewish life in Babylonia in general. However, when the discussion pertained to Babylonian Torah and its institutions, the content of their comments often became much more negative and their tone much sharper. Thus, for example, *b. Pes.* 34b relates the following:

> When Rabin went up [to the land of Israel] he repeated the teaching [of the Babylonian Sage Rav Sheshet] with reference to *terumah* plants before R. Jeremiah. Whereupon he observed: 'The Babylonians are fools. Because they dwell in a land of darkness they engage in dark discussions...'

The particulars of the teaching itself are not terribly important for our purposes. What is important, though, is that when a Babylonian teaching was recited before the fourth-century former Babylonian Sage R. Jeremiah, he responded with a biting attack on Babylonian Torah in general. R. Jeremiah's comment was not an isolated incident. Rather, he made a number of similar unfavorable comments regarding his former teachers, colleagues and friends from Babylonia and their Torah institutions. Thus in *b. Sanh.* 24a we find the following short but scathing comment:

> 'He hath made me to dwell in dark places like those that have long been dead' (Lam. 3.6). 'This', said R. Jeremiah, 'refers to the Babylonian Talmud'.

Similar comments were made by his teacher, R. Zeira, also a former Babylonian living and teaching in Palestine. Thus, it is related in *b. Meṣ* 85a that when R. Zeira went up from Babylonia to Palestine: 'He fasted a hundred fasts to forget the Babylonian *Gemara*, that it should not trouble him'.

Apparently it was not only the Babylonian *Gemara* which upset that Rabbi. R. Zeira in *b. Beṣ* 16a (= *b. Ned.* 49b) had the following to say about Babylonian culinary habits: 'The Babylonians are fools, eating bread with bread'. R. Zeira was referring to the Babylonian custom of eating solid food in a sandwich, which he found objectionable. He certainly, however, could have expressed his opinion without the insulting ethnic slight.

All in all, therefore, the Babylonians in Palestine had negative perceptions regarding their native land while hoping to fulfil their rabbinic and intellectual aspirations in their adopted country.

Babylonian Rabbis and Palestinian Society

The feelings and perceptions I have just described obviously did not exist within a vacuum. To succeed, these Babylonian Rabbis had to function in Palestinian society and indeed often at its highest levels. The reception afforded them by their host society could clearly affect their views regarding both Babylonia and Palestine and it is, therefore, necessary to determine how this reception influenced the views of these Babylonian immigrants and their attempts to break into Palestinian rabbinic circles.

The Babylonian rabbinical immigrants were under a good deal of pressure to succeed in Palestinian society and it is not unlikely that this pressure could have become a key element in the shaping of their personalities, and, therefore, also in the reception that their personalities may have evoked.[15] The success they sought, however, was not just a matter of a successful completion of their course of study. They also had to establish a successful interpersonal relationship with a teacher or master. Thus, the key to success was usually to study with such an important teacher or master and to forge a successful master–disciple relationship with him which would then provide access into Palestinian rabbinic society. In actuality, though, such relationships, in spite of their future promise, could also be fraught with danger. A master–disciple relationship could easily be perceived, by one side, at least, and probably that of the master, as a patron–client relationship with its own set of rules and obligations. This could prove a fertile ground for misunderstandings and tension, as we shall see below.[16] In any case, though, it is certainly not surprising that the more capable Babylonian Rabbis and students sought out the most prominent Palestinian

15. A good part of the Babylonian immigration to Palestine, composed of young Rabbis, sages or students, could be classified as 'student immigration' which is characterized by a strong, sometimes even obsessive, desire to succeed at their academic endeavors, since this was perceived as the key to successful professional integration. See, for example, R.G. Myers, *Education and Emigration* (New York: McKay, 1972) and F. Musgrove, *The Migratory Elite* (London: Heinemann, 1963).

16. See S.N. Eisenstadt and L. Roniger, *Patrons, Clients and Friends: Interpersonal Relations and the Structure of Trust in Society* (Cambridge: Cambridge University Press, 1984). On the honor and respect that the client owes the patron, see p. 213.

Rabbis such as the third century CE Sage, R. Johanan b. Ha-Napah.[17]

The ensuing relationships, were not, however always comfortable for either master or disciple. Sometimes it was a matter of different customs. In Palestine, for instance, the disciple was always careful to enquire about the health and welfare of his teacher. In Babylonia this was apparently less common.[18] Thus R. Eleazar b. Pedat, whom as we saw above was anti-Babylonia and aspired to success in Palestinian rabbinic circles, did not enquire after the health of his teacher R. Johanan when they met. R. Johanan was furious and referred to his disciple as 'that Babylonian'.[19] Was R. Eleazar trying so hard to be a Palestinian Rabbi because of this type of reaction, or perhaps in spite of this type of reaction?

R. Johanan's comment was not necessarily unique. Thus it was related in *y. Pes.* 5.32a that the Babylonian R. Simlai sought to study *aggadah* with the Palestinian Sage, R. Jonathan, who replied:

> It is a tradition from my fathers not to teach *aggadah* either to Babyloni-
> ans or Southerners [residents of Lydda in Judaea] because they are crass
> and ignorant of Torah, and you are from Nehardea [in Babylonia] and live
> in the South.[20]

17. The many Babylonian students who studied with this famous Rabbi included, for instance, R. Eleazar b. Pedat (*y. Ber.* 1.4b), Issi bar Hini (*b. Ḥul.* 137b), R. Zakkai (*y. Ṣab.* 7.9a), Zeiri (*b. Qid.* 71a), Hiyya bar Joseph (*b. Giṭ* 39a), Simeon b. Abba (*b. Ḥul.* 93a), Hiyya b. Abba (*b. Šab.* 105b), R. Hoshaiah II (*b. Sanh.* 14a), R. Haninah (*b. Sanh.* 14a), Ammi (*b. Ḥul.* 111b) and Assi (*b. Šab.* 45b).

18. See B. M. Levin, *Otzar Hiluf Minhagim bein Beney Eretz Yisrael uvein Beney Bavel* (Jerusalem: Mosad ha-Rav Kuk, photo-offset edition, 1972), p. 67: 'In the Land of Israel a student greets his teacher. In Babylonia a student does not greet his teacher.'

19. See *y. Šeq.* 2.47a. It is related that an elderly R. Johanan was walking on his way supported by his (Babylonian) student, R. Hiyya b. Abba. R. Eleazar saw them and did not greet his teacher. In addition to being angry with him over this, R. Johanan accused R. Eleazar of not citing teachings he had heard from him in his name. See also *b. Yeb.* 96b and *y. Ber.* 2.4b; *y. M. Qaṭ.* 3.83c and *Midrash Samuel* 19.4.

20. From the tradition it is apparent that there was not only an anti-Babylonian animus, but also an anti-Judean or Lyddan one. On this matter and on the combina-tion of negative feelings voiced for the most by Galilean Rabbis, see J. Schwartz, *Lod (Lydda), Israel: From its Origins through the Byzantine Period, 5600 BCE–640 CE* (British Archaeological Reports; International Series, 571; Oxford: Tempus Reparatum, 1991), p. 103; J. Schwartz, 'Southern Judaea and Babylonia', *JQR* 72 (1982), pp. 188-97.

Another tradition (*b. Yom.* 9b) tells of the Babylonian Sage Rabbah b. Bar Hannah who offered his hand to the third century CE Palestinian Rabbi, Resh Lakish, to help him out of the Jordan River after he had finished swimming there, and Resh Lakish refused to take his hand saying that 'God hated you [Babylonians]'. Resh Lakish was referring to the fact that most of the Babylonian Diaspora had elected to remain in Babylonia, where economic conditions were certainly better than those in Palestine, and had not moved to Palestine.[21]

The Babylonian Rabbis and students also had to suffer occasional insults, indignities and barbs from local non-elite or rabbinical circles[22] who probably saw their Babylonian accented Hebrew or Aramaic, their Babylonian dress and perhaps even their tendency to continue to eat Babylonian food in Palestine as convenient objects for attack and scorn.[23]

The Price of Success and Patriotism

How did all this affect the attitudes of these Babylonian immigrants to their new society? The fact is that the situation just described above may not have been as bad as one might have thought. In actuality there was not all that much differentiating the Babylonian Rabbis or students from their Palestinian compatriots. After all, they did speak the same Hebrew or Aramaic, in spite of different accents as already noted, and there were certainly no major theological points of contention or controversy between Babylonians and Palestinians. The

21. See L. Jacobs, 'The Economic Conditions of the Jews in Babylonia in Talmudic Times Compared with Palestine', *JSS* 2 (1957), pp. 349-59.

22. *y. Ber.* 2. 5c relates a number of such cases. Thus, for example, a rather young, but apparently quite capable, R. Kahana was accosted in Tiberias by an 'evil person' who mockingly asked the Babylonian Sage what heavenly voices he was hearing. R. Kahana returned to Babylonia on account of this encounter. R. Yassa [Assi], after having his hair cut, went to bathe in the hot springs of Tiberias and was struck by a local resident. R. Zeira, after undergoing blood-letting wished to buy some meat, but was informed by the butcher that he would have to endure a blow as part of the price.

23. On Babylonian accented Hebrew or Aramaic see *b. M. Qaṭ* 16b. On Babylonian clothes or fashions made by a weaver in Caesarea, see L. Levine, *Caesarea under Roman Rule* (SJLA, 7; Leiden: E.J. Brill, 1975), p. 270. On a Baylonian baker from Joppa see *CII*, II, p. 125, §902. It is not clear, though, whether he was actually baking Babylonian bread.

primacy of Torah, both Written and Oral, was certainly never a matter for discussion. It is doubtful, therefore, that the Babylonians had to suffer all that much of a 'culture shock' in Palestine.[24] Thus, the animosity described above should probably be seen more in terms of 'family squabbles' which might take on sharp tones, but certainly it should not be seen as either persecution or oppression.[25] At worst, the sources mentioned above could reflect 'hostile feelings', which often lie dormant in any case, or even if aggravated, often embody a degree of respect and admiration for the object of those feelings. These sources do not reflect aggressive power struggles or hatred-ridden conflicts between newcomers and natives.[26]

The plain fact is that the Babylonians did succeed in becoming important members of the Palestinian rabbinical hierarchy and, in spite of their talents or qualifications, they could never have done this if their Palestinian rabbinical colleagues had stonewalled them, or if the tension and 'hate' had been too great. On the contrary, and in spite of everything, the Palestinian Rabbis let them in.

However, admission to the upper echelons of Palestinian Rabbinic circles had its price. These Babylonians were not admitted as Babylonian Rabbis, but as Palestinian ones; or, in other words, the Palestinian Rabbis demanded of these Babylonians what is known as 'identificational assimilation' as opposed to 'structural assimilation'. The former is total and absolute identification. The latter is a more opportunistic variety whereby the level of identification is just enough to succeed.[27] The ultimate goal of the Palestinian hosts and the Baby-

---

24. See, for instance, G. Simmel, *Conflict and the Web of Group-Affiliation* (Illinois: Glencoe, 1955), pp. 43-45. There is a tendency to ignore common characteristics and feelings between immigrants and their host society and to accentuate only the negative.

25. Simmel, *Conflict*. See also S. Lieberman, '"That Is How It Was and That Is How It shall Be": The Jews of Eretz Israel and World Jewry During Mishnah and Talmud Times', *Cathedra* 17 (1980), pp. 3-10 (Hebrew). Cf. L.A. Coser, *The Functions of Social Conflict* (London: Routledge & Kegan Paul, 1956), p. 62. According to Coser, the closer relationships inherent in 'family squabbles' can result in increased attempts at reconciliation. Unfortunately, these often only increase tension instead of alleviating it.

26. On the differences between 'conflict' and 'hostile feelings' see Coser, *The Functions of Social Conflict*, pp. 37-40.

27. On these phrases see M.M. Gordon, *Assimilation in American Life* (New York: Oxford University Press, 1964), pp. 70-71. See also Musgrove, *The Migra-*

lonian success-seekers was 'institutional dispersion', whereby the Babylonians would receive positions in the Palestinian hierarchy without any reference whatsoever to their ethnic background, since this would to all intents and purposes disappear.[28]

All this brings me back to matters of identity and local patriotism. It is likely that a good deal of the violently anti-Babylonia comments of some of these Babylonian Rabbis in Palestine, as well as their overwhelming desire to become identified as Palestinian Rabbis, reflect the trend described above. These Rabbis were willing to pay the price of identificational assimilation in order to guarantee their success. Unfortunately for them, however, this was easier said than done, since there were often other forces at work.

Thus, adapting to a new country and surroundings can often prove to be a difficult challenge, even for extremely capable immigrants. It is not surprising, therefore, that immigrants tend to gravitate to one another and even to live together in their own enclaves.[29] Such a trend, however, would have hindered attempts at the very integration which certain of the Babylonians were seeking. It is, of course, impossible to determine where all individual Babylonians lived, but in general the Babylonians were no exception to the rule just mentioned and there were established Babylonian communities in most of the major cities of Roman period Palestine.[30] Even some of the most radical Babylonian assimilationists probably sought the comfort of familiar

---

tory Elite. Successful immigrants, and particularly students, are often quite adept at establishing social and professional contacts to aid them in their quests for success. These contacts, however, are often superficial and utilitarian. Perhaps R. Johanan suspected his disciple R. Eleazar b. Pedat of such motives when he reacted so violently to what he perceived as a slight by his student (see n. 19 above).

28. Cf. S.N. Eisenstadt, *The Absorption of Immigrants: A Comparative Study Based Mainly on the Jewish Community in Palestine and the State of Israel* (London: Routledge & Kegan Paul, 1954), p. 13.

29. On this trend in general, see, for example, E. Kane, 'Men and Kin in Donegal', *Ethnology* 7 (1968), p. 252; J. Wolper, 'Migration as an Adjustment to Environment Stress', *Journal of Social Issues* 22 (1966), pp. 92-102.

30. See, for instance, *Shir. R.* 8. 3: 'When Resh Lakish saw them [Babylonians] thronging the street [in Tiberias] he used to say to them: "when you went up [from exile] you would not form a crowd, and now do you come to form a crowd?"' Resh Lakish was upset with the Babylonians, who tended to 'throng together', although they did not do so some eight hundred years before during the period of restoration of Zion. On Babylonian communities in Sepphoris, Tiberias, Caesarea and Lydda, see Schwartz, 'Aliyah from Babylonia', pp. 63-64.

ethnic surroundings at some time or another.

All of this, however, was not the only force hindering the identificational assimilation of those who so desired it. An analysis of the halachic decisions of many of the Babylonian Rabbis in Palestine, even those such as R. Zeira who tried so hard to identify with Palestinian tradition, has revealed that they often introduced Babylonian elements or views into their decisions. It is possible that they may have not actually been aware of this and that they introduced these Babylonians customs on a subconscious level, but, be that as it may, it appears that many of these Rabbis could not disassociate themselves from their Babylonian homeland or traditions, in spite of how hard they tried.[31]

There were also matters of a personal nature which the Babylonian immigrants could not easily brush aside. Marriage into the host society is one of the highest levels of assimilation. Unfortunately, some of the Babylonians in Palestine were quite particular about their lineage, particularly in relation to marriage. Thus, *b. Qid.* 71b relates that the prominent Palestinian Sage, R. Johanan, offered the hand of his daughter to the Babylonian immigrant, Zeiri. This should be considered as the ultimate gesture of the host society to the newcomer aspiring to success. Zeiri, however, considered his Babylonian lineage 'purer' than that of his teacher and he turned him down![32]

---

31. See A. Goldberg, 'Palestinian Law in Babylonian Tradition, as Revealed in a Study of *Pereq 'Arvei Pesahim'*, *Tarbiz* 33 (1964), pp. 337-48 (Hebrew); A. Goldberg, 'Rabbi Zeira and Babylonian Custom', *Tarbiz* 36 (1967), pp. 319-41 (Hebrew). In the final analysis, though, this may have made it easier for the Babylonian Diaspora, Rabbis and lay community, to accept the halachic supremacy of the Torah center in Palestine. The large number of successful Babylonians in the Palestinian halachic hierarchy who, in spite of their best efforts, still remained Babylonian would make it appear to those Babylonians at home that they were actually accepting 'Babylonian' decisions and traditions, in spite of their geographic origin. On Babylonian recognition of this supremacy, see, for instance, *b. Pes.* 51a, *b. Ket.* 75a, *b. Men.* 42a and *b. Ta'an.* 21b.

32. The historical value of this tradition is probably somewhat minimal. Cf. S. Safrai, 'Tales of the Sages in the Palestinian Tradition and in the Babylonian Tradition', *Scripta Hierosolymitana* 22 (1971), p. 209. In any case, it is likely that if R. Johanan had a daughter, he would have offered her in marriage to someone like Zeiri, whom some have even identified with R. Zeira, mentioned a number of times above.

Summary

Many of the Babylonian immigrant Rabbis and students in Palestine espoused an enthusiastic brand of local Torah patriotism as part of a process of assimilation and acculturation. The process was not always successful. Most of these Rabbis at best reached a stage of structural assimilation. They became Palestinian enough to succeed and to be allowed to succeed, but remained Babylonian at the core, arousing resentment of the local population at all levels.[33] Their negative feelings regarding Babylonia may have indeed been real, but it was simply impossible for them to divorce themselves completely from their roots and past.

Ultimately, however, the failure of the Babylonians to integrate completely into Palestinian rabbinic society may have been beneficial for all concerned. The tension and resentment that the Babylonians aroused simply forced them to try harder to succeed and, subsequently, the Palestinians also had to work harder so as not to be outdone by the Babylonian newcomers and upstarts. The outstanding intellectual results of this tension and these efforts are well known in shaping the course of the history of Talmudic-period Judaism in both Palestine and Babylonia.

33. It is also important to remember that not every Babylonian Rabbi or student in Palestine came with the express purpose of remaining there. There were also many Babylonians who came for short-term visits or study periods and it is unlikely that they made much effort to assimilate. It is also likely that the local population could not always differentiate between short-term visitors and immigrants. On short-term Babylonian visitors or students see Schwartz, 'Aliyah from Babylonia', p. 63.

SYNAGOGUES OF THE HEBREWS: 'GOOD JEWS' IN THE DIASPORA

Graham Harvey

Among the Diaspora synagogues of classical antiquity at least two (one in Corinth and one in Rome) carried an inscription reading 'Synagogue of the Hebrews'. What did this mean to the people who paid for and erected the inscriptions? What was it intended to mean to those who saw it? What did it mean to the congregation who gathered in the building? Why are a number of deceased people remembered or named as 'Hebrews' rather than as 'Jews' or 'Israel'? Why did Jews of Aphrodisias feel the need to call themselves 'Hebrews' in graffiti on the seats of the odeum? What choices influenced the use of this appellation rather than another? What does the term 'Hebrew(s)' mean?

This chapter explores the meaning of such designations to members of these synagogues, to other Jews and to Gentiles. It will be argued that existing interpretations (e.g. that the congregation spoke Hebrew, that this was the first congregation established here, that the congregation was composed of first-generation immigrants or had come from Palestine, that it was a Samaritan synagogue) are problematic, and that the wider usage of the term 'Hebrew(s)' in ancient Jewish literature provides the context in which these inscriptions can be interpreted more adequately. Literature, such as the biblical sources, Josephus, Philo, the Mishnah and Christian writings, suggests that the term 'Hebrew(s)' is conventionally associated with loyalty, traditionalism, piety and conservatism; Hebrews are 'good Jews'. As a self-designation, 'Hebrew(s)' is a claim to be traditionally pious—it is moving towards an assertion that those so named are 'orthodox'. These conventional associations make it likely that the 'Synagogues of the Hebrews' were claiming to be the most representative Jewish congregations in the city. Although this conclusion can only be tentative it does provide a more convincing explanation than those which have been proposed in the past, and one which is grounded in the broader social and cultural context.

The Inscriptions[1]

The extant inscriptions in which the term 'Hebrew(s)' occur in Greek, Latin and Hebrew have minimal contextual evidence and permit a variety of interpretations. The following is a list of all known occurrences. All datable inscriptions are from the second to fifth centuries CE.

(1) *hic requiisquet* | *Numerius ebreus* | *qui bicset annos XX* (followed by figure indicating 6), | *cuius anima in req* | *ue.*
אמין עמרה (ethrog) (menorah) (shofar) שלום
Here rests Numerius the Hebrew, who lived 26 years, his spirit in rest. Peace. His dwelling place (?). Amen.
JIWE I.33 (pp. 52-53). Naples, fifth century CE.

(2) *hic requiṣ[cit] in pace Crescentia filia Pascasi ebrea* | *virgo qui vixit|annus p(lus) m(inus) XVIII.*
אמן.(menorah) שלום
Here rests in peace Crescentia daughter of Pascasus, the Hebrew woman, a virgin who lived more or less 18 years. Peace. Amen.
JIWE I.35 (p. 54). Naples, fifth century CE.

(3) (shofar) (menorah) (lulab) שלום
hic positus | *est Flaes ebr* | *eus.*
Peace. Here was placed Flaes the Hebrew.
JIWE I.37 (pp. 56-57). Naples, fourth–fifth century CE.

(4) ἐνθά<δ>ε κεῖτε | Γελάσις ἐξάρχων | τῶν Ἑβρέων· ἐν εἰρήνῃ ἡ κοίμησις αὐ—(menorah)—το—(amphora)—ῦ.
Here lies Gelasius, *exarchon* of the Hebrews. In peace his sleep.
JIWE II.2 (pp. 11-12). Monteverde, Rome, third–fourth century CE (?).

(5) [– –] ואסודרה ברת |
[– – Ἰσ] ιδώρα θυγά | [τηρ – –] ἄρχ (οντος) Ἑβρέων.
(Aramaic): Isidora, a daughter...
(Greek):... Isidora, daughter of... *archon* of the Hebrews...
JIWE II.33 (pp. 35-36). Monteverde, Rome: third–fourth century CE (?).

(6) (hedera) Ἰουλιανὸς (hedera) | (hedera) Ἑβρέος. (hedera)
Julianus, a Hebrew.
JIWE II.44 (pp. 42-43). Monteverde, Rome, third–fourth century CE (?).

(7) Μόνιμός ὁ καὶ Εὐ | σαββάτις Ἑβραῖος | καὶ γλυκὺς ἔζη—(hedera) | σεν ἔτη δ<έ>κα | ICA [ ]IZ.
Monimus who (was) also (called) Eusabbatis, Hebrew and dear, lived ten (?)

1. Dotted underlining indicates an uncertain reading.

years...

JIWE II.108 (pp. 91-92). Monteverde, Rome, third–fourth century CE (?).

(8) ἐνθάδε κῖτε | Μακεδόνις | ὁ Αἰβρέος Κεσαρεὺς | τῆς Παλεστίνης, | υἱὸς Ἀλεξάνδρου· || μνία δικαίου εἰς | εὐλογίαν· ἐν ἰρή | νη ἡ κοίμισί<ς> σου.

Here lies Macedonius the Hebrew from Caesarea in Palestine, son of Alexander. The memory of the righteous one for a blessing. In peace your sleep.

JIWE II.112 (p. 95). Monteverde, Rome, third–fourth century CE (?).

(9) ἐνθάδε κεῖτε | Καίλις Κυεῖντ | ος φιλοπάτωρ | β΄ ἄρχων ἐτῶν ι<γ> | παῖς Ἑ[β]ραῖος (hedera)

Here lies Caelius Quintus, who loved his father, *archon* for the second time, aged 13 (?), a Hebrew boy.

JIWE II.559 (pp. 443-44). Unknown provenance, third–fourth century CE (?).

(10) Ἀλύπις Τιβερεὺς καὶ υἱ | οἱ αὐτοῦ Ἰοῦστος | καὶ Ἀλύπις Ἑβρε | οι μετὰ τοῦ πατρὸς | αὐτῶν ὧδε κῖντε.

Alypius of Tiberias and his sons Justus and Alypius, Hebrews, with their father, lie here.

JIWE II.561 (pp. 445-46). Unknown provenance, second–fourth century CE (?).

(11) ὧδε κεῖ | τε Σαλὼ | θυγάτηρ Γα | δία πατρὸς | συναγωγῆς || Αἰβρέων· ἐβί | ωσεν (ἔτη) μα· | ἐν εἰρήνη | ἡ κοίμη | σεις αὐτῆς.

Here lies Salo, daughter of Gadias, father of the synagogue of the Hebrews. She lived 41 years. In peace her sleep.

JIWE II.578 (pp. 459-60). Unknown provenance, third–fourth century CE (?).

(12) ἐντάδε κῖτε | τυγατέρες δύο | πατρὸς τῶν | Ἑβρέων Γα | δίατος· Κάρα ἐν ἰ || ρήνη.

Here lie the two daughters of (the) father of the Hebrews, Gadias. Cara, in peace.

JIWE II.579 (pp. 460-61). Rome or Porto: third-fourth century CE (?).

(13a) Seating block d, row 6:

Τόπος Βενέτων

Ἑβρέων τῶν παλειῶν.

Place of the Blues;

for the Hebrew Elders.

(13b) Seating block b, row 5:

Τόπος Ἑβρέων.

Place of the Hebrews.

JGA, p. 132. Graffiti on seating in the odeum of Aphrodisias, late sixth century CE (?).

(14) [...] \ΓΩΓΗΕΒΡ[...]

Reconstructed as [Συνα]γωγὴ ἑβρ[αίων].

Synagogue of the Hebrews.

CII I.718 (p. 518). Corinth. First–third century CE (?).

The Meanings of 'Meaning'

How can the meaning of 'Hebrew(s)' in these inscriptions (which will be taken to include the graffiti from Aphrodisias) be determined? There is little or nothing in the inscriptions themselves to tell us how those who ordered them, carved them or saw them, understood the name.

We might assume that 'Hebrews' are speakers of the language called Hebrew. Since the Aramaic language is sometimes called 'Hebrew',[2] we might widen this to include Aramaic speakers. However, notwithstanding the occasional phrase or word of Hebrew or Aramaic in the inscriptions, David Noy correctly points out that 'there is no clear connection with the Hebrew language'.[3] The reading 'speaker of a language' would not make sense in any of these predominantly Greek and Latin inscriptions.

Abandoning presuppositions based on our current usage of the word 'Hebrew', and asking only what the texts tell us, provides very limited information. Men, women and children are called 'Hebrews'. They are clearly Jewish: they use Jewish texts (e.g. inscription 8 uses Aquila's version of Prov. 10.7),[4] they use Jewish symbols and most come from Jewish locations. But we already know that 'Hebrew' is closely related to, or even synonymous with, 'Jew' and 'Israel'. What the inscriptions do not tell us is why they do not use these other designations. Indeed, one of them, 'Israel', is rarely used as an individual designation in inscriptions.[5] Thus, an examination of what is explicit or readily apparent in the inscriptions tells us little of value about the name 'Hebrew(s)' and therefore about the self-understanding of those who use it.

---

2. For example, in *Ant.* 1.33, 34 Josephus says that the Aramaic σάββατα means 'rest', κατὰ τὴν ἑβραίων διάλεκτον. See also Jn 5.2; 19.13, 17; 20.16.

3. *JIWE* II, p. 12. Also see J.Z. Smith, 'Fences and Neighbours: Some Contours of Early Judaism', in W.S. Green (ed.), *Approaches to Ancient Judaism* (Chico, CA: Scholars Press, 1980), II, pp. 1-25 (19), who supports Frey, *CII*, I, p. lxxvi against A. Momigliano, 'I nomi delle prime "sinagoghe" romane e la condizione giuridica della communità in Roma sotto Augusto', *Rassegna Mensile di Israël* 6 (1931), pp. 283-92, especially pp. 290-92.

4. *JIWE* II, p. 95.

5. See the indexes in *JIWE* I and II, and similar collections of ancient Jewish inscriptions.

It would be ideal for the purpose of this discussion if the name 'Hebrew' could be shown, simply and without doubt, to refer to an assertion of relationship with the land of Israel. But, regrettably, stating that 'Hebrews' were 'people whose Diaspora identity was focused on a patriotic assertion of the importance of their origins in Palestine' is not so straightforward. Only inscriptions 8 and 10 clearly refer to Palestine, but even these do not suggest that this region defines the meaning of 'Hebrew'. While no other 'Hebrews' are said to be from Palestine, another Caesarean is not designated a 'Hebrew'.[6] Furthermore, with respect to inscription 10, the names Alypius and Justus may have been common in Tiberias, but there is no evidence that 'Hebrew' was more favoured as a designation than any other in Tiberias or elsewhere in Galilee.[7] If 'Hebrew' is, as Smith claims, 'an ethno-geographical [designation which] indicates that one's place of birth was in Syro-Palestine from which the individual emigrated to Rome',[8] this is not evident from the inscriptions. If it is true, evidence for it must be found elsewhere.

I have assumed until now that 'meaning' can best be ascertained by examining the immediate context of a word, or by exploring the field of words associated with it, that is, the textual context. In this way it is possible to detect shifts in the meaning of the same word in different contexts depending on its associations. Another, contrasting, approach, frequently adopted in the analysis of biblical and other ancient texts, is to seek the meaning of words in their formal similarity to others. Thus, a relationship is asserted between words that look or sound similar, sometimes in other languages. Even if this is a matter of cognate languages, however, this approach still does not provide us with the meaning of a word, only its possible history.[9] A discussion of the etymology of the term 'Hebrew' would, in short, tell us nothing useful

6.   *JIWE* II, p. 459.

7.   See *JIWE* II, pp. 445-46 for references to other Jews named Alypius and Justus and for a Jew from Sepphoris who is not named 'Hebrew'.

8.   Smith, 'Fences and Neighbours', p. 19. Also see P. Richardson, *Israel in the Apostolic Church* (Cambridge: Cambridge University Press, 1969), p. 118 and n. 2.

9.   J. Barr, *The Semantics of Biblical Language* (Oxford: Oxford University Press, 1961), p. 109. Also see J.F.A. Sawyer, *Semantics in Biblical Research: New Methods of Defining Hebrew Words for Salvation* (London: SCM Press, 1972) and J. Riches, *Jesus and the Transformation of Judaism* (London: Darton, Longman & Todd, 1980).

about its function in these inscriptions.

Those few passages of ancient Jewish literature that do indulge in a kind of etymology might be seen to offer some support to the contention that 'Hebrews' are those who have left Palestine to settle in Rome or elsewhere. LXX Gen. 14.13 calls Abram ὁ περάτης rather than Ἑβραῖος. However, the translators derived this reading from the consonant sequence עבר rather than from the designation עברי: that is, 'migrant' is to be understood as an appellative unconnected to the gentilic.[10] Philo claims that the name 'Hebrew' means 'Migrant' (περάτης), which he interprets as 'quitting sense perceptions to go after those of Mind'.[11] Some Christian writers follow Philo's usage and sermonize on 'Hebrews' as those who 'crossed boundaries'.[12] These references to journeys, pilgrimage and development are, however, not only infrequent in Jewish and Christian writings, but the majority of them do not interpret 'Hebrews', playing rather with the consonant sequence.

If the attempt to find meaning in the putative history or origins of a word is inadequate and the immediate context of the word tells us little of value, as in this case, how can we gain greater precision in our interpretation of the word 'Hebrew'? Is there any other way of exploring the semantic, or associative field of the term as it occurs in these Roman period Diaspora inscriptions? It has been asserted that 'Hebrew' is a word that Jews use in reference to themselves, or to other Jews when non-Jews are in view—usually in literary contexts. This is the centrepiece of Tomson's argument about the meaning of the name in ancient Jewish and early Christian literature and is also occasionally asserted by Stern in discussing early rabbinic literature.[13] It might also be applied in the case of the inscriptions which were placed in relatively or completely public places where non-Jews would see them. However, we do not know whether this was the case, nor are we helped in our quest for understanding. The theory does not tell

10. G. Harvey, *The True Israel* (Leiden: E.J. Brill, 1996), p. 111.

11. Philo, *Migr. Abr.* 20.

12. References in N. de Lange, *Origen and the Jews: Studies in Jewish–Christian Relations in Third Century Palestine* (Cambridge: Cambridge University Press, 1976), p. 36.

13. P.J. Tomson, 'The Names Israel and Jew in Ancient Judaism and in the New Testament', *Bijdragen, Tijdschrift Voor Filosofie en Theologie* 47 (1986), pp. 120-40, 266-89 and S. Stern, *Jewish Identity in Early Rabbinic Writings* (Leiden: E.J. Brill, 1994).

us what either Jews or non-Jews were meant to understand by the word, but only asserts that presumably it made some sense to them. Contrary to this theory, there is plenty of literary evidence that Jews and non-Jews were quite happy to use the names 'Jew', 'Israel' and 'Hebrew' (undoubtedly with different associations at different times). In short, the 'insiders versus outsiders' distinction is not derived from the usage of the names, but from an unconfirmed theory.[14]

In the remainder of this discussion I provide an overview of the occurrences of 'Hebrew' in extant ancient Jewish and early Christian literature. Whilst this cannot prove that the buyers, carvers or viewers of the inscriptions understood 'Hebrew' to have exactly the same meaning, it does reveal that the name had carried certain conventional associations for a long time. These conventional associations would make perfect sense in an inscriptional context, unlike the assertion that 'Hebrews' are 'Jews seen from an outsider's perspective' or that 'Hebrews, therefore, usually were to be found in Palestine and only rarely in the Diaspora'.[15]

'Hebrews' in Ancient Literature

The 'language' of those who dedicated synagogues and honoured their dead is that of a wider religious tradition, of the Bible and of Judaism. Even translated into Latin and Greek this religious language resonated with a strong tradition of conventional usage. In the Bible (in Hebrew and Greek) 'Hebrews' are those who assert their links to Abraham, the first 'Hebrew' (Gen. 14.13), and thus to traditional piety. עברים occurs at:

> Gen. 14.13; 39.14,17; 40.15; 41.12; 43.32.
> Exod. 1.15,16,19; 2.6,7,11,13; 3.18; 5.3; 7.16; 10.3; 21.2.
> Deut. 15.12.
> 1 Sam. 4.6,9; 13.3,7,19; 14.11,21; 29.3.
> Jer. 34.9,14.
> Jon. 1.9.

The name is used to label some of the most important people and some

---

14. See Harvey, *The True Israel*, for Jewish and Christian uses; and M. Stern, *Greek and Latin Authors on Jews and Judaism* (3 vols.; Jerusalem: Israel Academy of Sciences, 1974–1984) for Gentile authors.

15. W.L. Moran, 'Hebrews', in William J. McDonald (ed.), *New Catholic Encyclopedia* (Catholic University of America, 1967), VI, p. 978.

of the earliest generations in the story of Israel. It is associated with antiquity, origins and people of central importance.[16]

Jonah provides an excellent example of its use and associations. When asked by foreign sailors who he is, Jonah identifies himself as a 'Hebrew'. The author's careful use of words in this work[17] suggests that עברי was deliberately chosen here, but it is not immediately obvious what Jonah's reply means. Allen's explanation that 'Jonah answers the last question first, explaining that he is a Hebrew, the term generally used by the people of Israel in describing themselves to foreigners'[18] is inadequate as this is a text written not for foreigners, but for 'insiders'. Beyond avoiding the potential inaccuracy of having an allegedly northern Israelite reply, 'I am a Judean',[19] 'Hebrew' adds to the '"old world" air' of the book,[20] and is linked with the phrase 'God of the Hebrews' (Exod. 3.18). Allen states, 'this means that Jonah is a worshipper of Yahweh', although Jonah's actual behaviour belies this claim to be one who 'fears' his God.[21] The writer has Jonah use this name rather than any other because it is associated with such 'archaic' figures as Abraham and with the God of the Exodus. It highlights the irony of Jonah's attempt to flee from God whilst the sailors are actually afraid of God. Jonah's 'orthodoxy', or piety is a front, a thin disguise.

Biblical uses of 'Hebrew' include references to 'Hebrew slaves'. עבד עברים and עבריות (Exod. 21.2; Deut. 15.12-15; Jer. 34.9) were Israelites who had been enslaved, not foreigners enslaved by Israelites. The obvious difficulty, that this contradicts the legislation of Lev. 25.39-40, is not solved within the text and remains a problem. This usage of 'Hebrew' is productive of occurrences in Josephus and in the Mishnah, but it is clearly quite a distinct and specific use of the term. Josephus refers to the 'Hebrew slave' law at *Ant.* 4.273, but avoids naming such slaves Ἑβραῖοι in this context because the name had strongly positive associations. It was not to be linked to slavery, but

16. There are some additional occurrences in LXX and the Samaritan Pentateuch, but their associations are identical to those noted.

17. J. Magonet, *Form and Meaning: Studies in Literary Techniques in the Book of Jonah* (Bern: Peter Lang, 1976).

18. L.C. Allen, *The Books of Joel, Obadiah, Jonah and Micah* (London: Hodder & Stoughton, 1976), p. 209.

19. Although Jonah intends to return to the Temple (2.5; RSV 2.4).

20. Allen, *The Books*, p. 176.

21. Allen, *The Books*, p. 209.

with the Laws, constitution and virtues of the 'Hebrew nation' from the time of Moses up until Josephus's own time. The 'nation' in this summary predates the giving of the Law and the name 'Hebrew(s)' bears strong associations with the nation's origins and virtue.

In the Mishnah's system, 'Hebrew slaves' are significant as anomalous Israelites.[22] Its interest is in the role of these anomalous characters—there is no need to assume or deny their actual existence—in unusual situations. The question addressed is whether 'Hebrew slaves' are more like independent, autonomous people (landowning, male, heads of families) or more like their wives and children. They are distinguishable from 'Canaanite slaves' not primarily by race, but by status in this system: for 'Canaanite' read 'permanent', for 'Hebrew' read 'indentured servant'.[23] In some circumstances some people (wives, widows of brothers, minor children, Canaanite slaves) can only act as extensions of the autonomous individual but other people (adult children, perhaps divorced wives) can act independently. As members of 'Israel', but lacking independence, the concept of 'Hebrew slaves' provides a means of exploring these anomalous situations. The Mishnah's purpose is not to describe or legislate for actual 'Hebrew slaves', but to elaborate and explore such anomalous situations and the distinctions which arise from them. The *Tosefta* (which refers to 'Hebrew slaves' eleven times)[24] makes one additional point without challenging the Mishnah's assumptions and interests. It distinguishes between people by gender: 'Hebrew slaves' are male, not female; the piercing of a slave's ear with an awl refers to men, not women; and 'Hebrew slaves' can be owned by men, not women.[25]

These 'Hebrew slaves' and the issues that centre on them in biblical literature, Josephus and Rabbinic literature, have only one thing in common with the inscriptions of interest to us: they are Israelites. It seems self-evident that synagogue and funerary inscriptions would not draw attention to the misfortune of the occupants in being or having

---

22. *m. B. Qam.* 8.3; *m. Qid.* 1.2; *m. Ma'as. Š.* 4.4; *m. 'Erub.* 7.6; *m. B. Meṣ* 1.5; *m. 'Arak.* 8.5; J. Neusner, *The Mishnah: A New Translation* (New Haven: Yale University Press, 1988). See also P.V. Flescher, *Oxen, Women, or Citizens? Slaves in the System of the Mishnah* (Atlanta: Scholars Press, 1988) and G.G. Porten, *Goyim: Gentiles and Israelites in Mishnah–Tosefta* (Atlanta: Scholars Press, 1988).

23. Flescher, *Oxen, Women, or Citizens?*, p. 54.

24. J. Neusner, *The Tosefta: An Introduction* (Atlanta: Scholars Press, 1992).

25. *t. Soṭ.* 2.9 and *m. Soṭ.* 3.8 share this interest in gender but do not refer to 'Hebrew slaves'.

been slaves or indentured servants. It is equally clear that the flavour of the inscriptions is very different from that of the slavery literature, which can, therefore, be ignored in this attempt to understand who the 'Hebrews' of the inscriptions were.

In the texts now generally labelled Apocrypha and Pseudepigrapha 'Hebrew(s)' functions as the name of the people and of the language. References to the language need not detain us, other than noting by way of example that *Jubilees* considers Abram (12.26, 27) and Joseph (43.15) to be speakers of the holy Hebrew language. The 'Hebrews' of 2 Maccabees,[26] Judith,[27] *4 Maccabees*,[28] and *3 Sibylline Oracles*[29] are pious and traditional members of a nation persecuted precisely for its piety and its relationship with God. In 2 Maccabees, Ἑβραῖος even 'acts as a synonym designating the Jews who participated in the Maccabean revolt'.[30] The actions of foreigners provoke a situation where it is obvious which people are firm in their adherence to ancestral traditions. In so doing, a 'Jew' or 'Israel' is shown to be a 'Hebrew'. Ἑβραῖος is a synonym of Ἰουδαῖος, or Ἰσραήλ, which is chosen not because it is an outsider's designation, but because it stresses the traditional virtues, or 'piety', of those so labelled and portrays those who rebel as standing in a long tradition of refusing to bow to foreigners. The name is part of the language of a theology of suffering and liberation.

The only occurrences of 'Hebrew' in all the literature found near the Dead Sea are in a copy of Jon. 1.9 at Murabba'at (Mur 88 x.14)[31] and in a Nahal Ḥever letter from Soumaios,[32] possibly Bar Kochba, which says that 'a [des]ire has not be[en] found to w[ri]te in Hebrew', ἑβραεστι (lines 11-15). The fragmentary state of the Qumran scrolls has obviously led to this lack of other references in biblical scrolls. Absence of 'Hebrew' as a self-designation among a group who considered themselves thoroughly pious may also be an unfortunate result of

26. 2 Macc. 7.31; 11.13 and 15.37.

27. Jdt. 10.12; 12.11; 14.18.

28. *4 Macc.* 4.11; 5.2,4; 9.5,18; 12.7; 16.15; 17.9.

29. *3 Sibylline Oracle*, pp. 68-76.

30. M. Gray, 'The Habiru–Hebrew Problem in the Light of the Source Material Available at Present', *HUCA* 29 (1958), pp. 135-97 (189).

31. DJD II, 183-90.

32. B. Lifshitz, 'Papyrus grecs du désert du Juda', *Aegyptus* 42 (1962), pp. 240-56; J. Fitzmyer, *A Wandering Aramean: Collected Aramaic Essays* (Missoula, MT: Scholars Press, 1979), pp. 35-36.

decay. Any other, more ideological, reason for its absence must remain purely hypothetical.

Philo's 'Hebrews' are speakers of the Hebrew (or Aramaic) language, an ancestral language, in distinction from the use of 'Greek' by other people of similar descent. When he says that the Ἑβραῖοι have a name for something,[33] Philo is not usually thinking of a specific generation, but is speaking inclusively ('this has always been and continues to be the name for x'). Philo also uses 'Hebrew' of the ancestors of the people, especially those so named in his (biblical?) sources and, almost without exception, those of the pre-conquest generation. The term 'Hebrews' in Philo's writings refers to respected and traditional people. For example, Philo notes that although Moses is called an 'Egyptian', Αἰγύπτιον, by Jethro's daughters (Exod. 2.19) he 'was not only a Hebrew, but was also of the purest Hebrew blood which alone is consecrated' (*Mut. Nom.* 117).

Josephus' use of 'Hebrews' is as a label for those related to the 'good' ancestors and ancestral traditions. For example, at *Ant.* 2.268 God tells Moses (from the burning bush) that he will be the leader of the 'Hebrew hosts, for they shall dwell where Abraham lived, the forefather of your race'. Josephus also uses Ἑβραῖοι for contemporary Jews and, most significantly, he himself is Ἑβραῖος (*War* 1.3). This latter usage is found in the preface to his account of the 'War between the Romans and the Ἰουδαῖοι', which he claims to have written because others have vilified the ''Ιουδαῖοι'. He does not consistently distinguish between Ἰουδαῖος and Ἑβραῖος in his works; anyone he calls by one name he will call by the other at another point.[34] Yet here he chooses to use a name not so immediately associated with the war. Later in his account of the war he says that the rebels have caused the disparaging of τὸ γένος τῶν Ἑβραῖων by their atrocities in Jerusalem.[35] By the use of different names Josephus wants to demonstrate that the whole nation is not to be implicated in whatever barbarities are attributable to the revolutionaries. The 'Hebrews' are 'good' people and the name is a positive one; however, the action of the revolutionaries has besmirched them and their name. Josephus's 'Hebrews' are 'good Jews'.

That the 'Hebrews' of early Christian literature are also 'good Jews'

33. E.g. *Abr.* 17, 28, 57; *Spec. Leg.* 2.41, 86; *Somn.* 2.250.
34. Cf. *Ant.* 7.101 and 105.
35. *War* 5.443.

can be demonstrated by brief reference to several typical texts. As the name of a group of people, 'Hebrew' only occurs four times in the New Testament.[36] It refers to the Hebrew language a further eleven times,[37] and it gains in popularity in other early Christian texts. 'Hebrews' occurs in 2 Cor. 11.22 and Phil. 3.5 in Paul's defence of his ministry against 'false apostles' and 'super apostles'. He denies he is innovative, or anything but a traditionalist, and claims that what he teaches is in continuity with biblical tradition. His gospel is not foreign to Jewish tradition, as he understands and presents it. What he dismisses as 'refuse' (Phil. 3.9) is all of these otherwise positive things as marks of his own special status. He does not deny their goodness in their (past) context. They are, however, no longer taxic indicators[38] of his kind of Judaism, that is, what soon became called Christianity. Paul's claim to be a 'Hebrew' adds to his claim to be an 'Israelite' (2 Cor. 11.22) and a 'Jew' (Gal. 1.13,14). As with other 'Hebrews', Paul claims (whatever the historical truth may be) to be a pious, loyal and traditional observer of ancestral ways.

Acts 6.1 refers to a difference of approach by 'Hellenists' and 'Hebrews'. A vast edifice has been built on this flimsy foundation. I suggest that the assumption that the difference between 'Hebrews' and 'Hellenists' is generative of the continuing narrative of Acts 6, 7 and 8 (as most commentators seem to assume) be abandoned. Stephen is not necessarily a 'Hellenist', or a 'Hebrew'. His speech is not necessarily representative of the 'Hellenists', or the 'Hebrews'. It may just be that all we are being told is that the dominant (at least in this situation) Hebrew or Aramaic speaking group did not understand (or want to understand) the needs of the Greek-speaking group. In other words, if we are to choose a title for Acts 6.1-6 it would not be, 'The Hebrews and Hellenists' but 'The Choice of the Seven'. The establishment of the 'Seven', enabling the church's rapid growth, acts as a prelude to the concern of these chapters with the persecution of the Church by 'the Jews' and that is another story. What is at issue is obviously not ideology but approach. Little more certainty can be gained about the

36. Acts 6.1; 2 Cor. 11.22; Phil. 3.5 and in the title of the Letter to the Hebrews.

37. Luke 23.38; Jn 5.2; 19.13, 17, 20; 20.16; Acts 21.40; 22.2; 26.14; Rev. 9.11; 16.16. The occurrence of ἑβραικοῖς at Lk. 23.38 is a gloss dependent on John.

38. Smith, 'Fences and Neighbours'.

meaning of 'Hebrews' in Acts 6.[39]

The titles of the 'Letter to the Hebrews' and the later *Gospel to the Hebrews* are of a piece with wider Christian usage in which 'Hebrews' are 'good Jews', but 'Jews' are 'opponents of God, Christ and the Church'. Those who wished to find an apt title for Christian documents obviously addressed to Christians to whom 'Jewish' traditions about Sinai and the wilderness were important, could not use 'Letter to the Jews', or 'Letter to Jewish Christians'. These would have carried negative associations while, conversely, 'Hebrews' was associated with faithful adherence to traditional virtues (whatever they were thought to be). Similarly, Clement refers to the Jerusalem Church in the time of James as 'the church of the Hebrews in Jerusalem', that is, 'loyal Jews'.[40] Christian tradition rapidly rejected the idea of their Jewish contemporaries being 'good', and increasingly used 'Hebrews' only to refer to 'good Jews' of the past, such as Abraham, David and Isaiah. For instance, in the middle of the second century CE Melito of Sardis accused 'Israel' of deicide, and highlighted this accusation by stressing the positive aspects of the location of this act:

> An unprecedented murder has occurred in the middle of Jerusalem,
> the city of the law,
> in the city of the Hebrews,
> in the city of the prophets,
> in the city accounted just.[41]

Whilst Melito was vehemently against Judaism, he believed that there were once 'good Jews' whom he referred to as 'Hebrews'.

If Jesus' Jewishness is now a cause of celebration and a double-edged opening for some Christians to engage in dialogue with Jews, it was once seen as adding to the culpability of 'his own who knew him not' (Jn 1.11). However, some Jews obviously did 'receive him', so it could be said that Jesus was 'born of a Hebrew maiden' and 'of the tribe of the Hebrews'.[42] Chrysostom says that Paul was wise to speak

39. I discuss this more fully in Harvey, *The True Israel*, pp. 132-36.

40. M. Black, *The Scrolls and Christian Origins* (London: Thomas Nelson, 1961), pp. 78, 79.

41. S. Hall (ed.), *Melito of Sardis on Pascha and Fragments* (Oxford: Oxford University Press, 1979), pp. 693-95. It is possible that the three appellations of 'the city' refer to the three divisions of the Bible in their Christian form: Law, Histories and Prophets. This would make 'Hebrews' a reference to the 'Historians'.

42. Syriac and Armenian version of the *Apology of Aristides*, para. 2 (Syriac).

to 'those who used the Greek tongue', ἑλληνιστι φθεγγομένους, because 'those others, those profound Hebrews had no mind even to see him'.[43] 'Hebrews' here has an honorific meaning, signifying something like 'conservative', 'traditional' or (given Chrysostom's anti-Judaism) 'good Jews'.[44] The early Syriac *Homily* 8 of the Pseudo-Clementines says that 'Jesus is hidden from the Jews, who have taken Moses as their teacher, and Moses is hidden from those who have believed Jesus'. This is not a condemnation, but a statement that 'God accepts him who has believed either of these'. The 'Hebrews' will not be 'condemned on account of their ignorance of Jesus...if, doing the things commanded by Moses, they do not hate him whom they do not know'. Nor will (Christian) Gentiles be condemned for ignorance of Moses if they obey Jesus.[45] Further examples from Christian literature could be adduced, but all make the same point: 'Hebrews' are 'good Jews'.

This overview and survey of the use of 'Hebrews' in ancient Jewish and early Christian literature has shown that the name consistently carries associations with piety, traditionalism and conservatism. It remains to return to the inscriptions in which the name occurs and ask if these conventional associations are evident there too.

Conclusion

Self-designations 'mean' something to those who hear or read them because they resonate with conventional associations and because they bear strong connotations that are not easily changed. Drawing on such associations and connotations, they speak to those who know the language, but are meaningless to others. Such public inscriptions as those which are of interest here can be assumed to have been intended to address someone. They are akin to puns and jokes in that their richness and impact depends on knowledge of the language and they become empty when explained.

The evidence adduced for the name's conventional associations indicates that 'Hebrews' are 'good Jews' in that they are traditional, pious and conservative. It is probable that the synagogues 'of the Hebrews'

43. John Chrysostom, *Homily* 21 on Acts 9.29.
44. The personal name in *JIWE* I, p. 35 makes it just possible that this is the inscription of a Jewish convert to Christianity: a 'very good Jew'.
45. *Homily* 8.6-7.

were asserting their conservatism, perhaps even their 'orthodoxy'. The inscriptions may have been obscure to passers-by, but not necessarily any more obscure than anything else in relation to the building or its users. It might, however, have suggested to those well-disposed towards Jews that the building belonged to people who were loyal to ancestral traditions and not radical innovators. Passers-by were not, of course, common in the catacombs. Here it is clear that something more than just 'Jewish' or 'Israelite' is meant by 'Hebrew'. The use of Palestinian place names (Caesarea and Tiberias) makes it less rather than more likely that 'Hebrew' refers to geographical origins. If the name clearly referred to 'Palestine' it would be unnecessary to inscribe, 'someone from Palestine, from Caesarea in Palestine'.[46] Reference to wider associations might permit a more 'educated guess' than that 'Jewish communities in [Rome,] Greece and Asia Minor also designated themselves [synagogue of the Hebrews]' because they were the first (Palestinian) Jewish community in their area.[47] Neither the dead nor the living were identified by the language they spoke to one another, or to their deity, but by their claim to conservative piety.

Conservatism, particularly religious conservatism, was highly valued in Roman society. While the 'Hebrews' of the Apocrypha might have expressed their piety by fighting foreigners, Josephus provides a lead in calling for a more quietist piety. The Mishnah travels the same road, clearly a much safer one for a minority people which has already lost two wars disastrously.[48] While it is impossible to prove any particular meaning for 'Hebrew' in these inscriptions beyond all possible doubt, it is likely that it does express a Josephus-style commitment to Rome rather than a Maccabean-style opposition to foreign rule.

These inscriptions affirm both Jewish religious identity and a commitment to the good of their new home. If passers-by were aware of the history of hostility between Romans and Jews and conversant with the language or systems of Judaism they might have noted that

---

46. Cf. P.W. van der Horst, *Ancient Jewish Epitaphs: An Introductory Survey of a Millennium of Jewish Funerary Epigraphy (300 BCE–700 CE)* (Kampen: Kok, 1991), pp. 69-70 and J.W. van Henten, 'A Jewish Epitaph in a literary text: 4 Macc. 17.8-10', in J.W. van Henten and P.W. van der Horst (eds.), *Studies in Early Jewish Epigraphy* (Leiden: E.J. Brill, 1994), pp. 44-69 (52).

47. Van der Horst, *Ancient Jewish Epitaphs*, pp. 87-88.

48. J. Neusner, *Judaism and its Social Metaphors: Israel in the History of Jewish Thought* (Cambridge: Cambridge University Press, 1989).

these were synagogues of good citizens rather than religious zealots. In terms beloved of the media today they were 'liberals' rather than 'fundamentalists'. They were pious Jews living a quiet life in their adopted cities, whose relatives affirmed that piety in permanent burial engravings when they died. They were respectable citizens of their cities, elders of their communities, loyal to their ancestral traditions and leading the kind of lives which they hoped would guarantee the survival of their people. The identity of these 'Hebrews' is an expression of a double loyalty: to Judaism and to citizenship, or at least patriotism towards their current home. These were not 'Palestinian Jews', wherever they came from, they were not zealots or visitors. The 'Hebrews' of Aphrodisias, Corinth, Naples and Rome were Diaspora Jews and, as such, in their view, they were 'good Jews'.

INDEXES

INDEX OF REFERENCES

OLD TESTAMENT

PSEUDEPIGRAPHA AND OTHER ANCIENT SOURCES

MISHNAH AND TALMUD

INDEX OF AUTHORS

JOURNAL FOR THE STUDY OF THE PSEUDEPIGRAPHA
SUPPLEMENT SERIES

DATE DUE